D0288640

From My Mother's Back

OTHER TITLES BY NJOKI WANE

*A Handbook on African Traditional Healing Approaches & Research
Practices*
Indigenous African Knowledge Production
Ruptures: Anti-colonial & Anti-racist Feminist Theorizing
Spiritual Discourse in the Academy

From My Mother's Back

A Journey from Kenya to Canada

Njoki Wane

WOLSAK
& WYNN

© Njoki Wane, 2020

No part of this publication may be reproduced, stored in a retrieval system or transmitted, in any form or by any means, without the prior written consent of the publisher or a license from the Canadian Copyright Licensing Agency (Access Copyright). For an Access Copyright license, visit www.accesscopyright. ca or call toll free to 1-800-893-5777.

Cover and interior design: Marijke Friesen
Cover images: iStock and Njoki Wane
Author photograph: Njoki Wane
Typeset in Caslon Book
Printed by Ball Media, Brantford, Canada

10 9 8 7 6 5 4 3 2 1

The publisher gratefully acknowledges the support of the Ontario Arts Council, the Canada Council for the Arts and the Government of Canada.

Wolsak and Wynn Publishers
280 James Street North
Hamilton, ON
Canada L8R 2L3

Library and Archives Canada Cataloguing in Publication

Title: From my mother's back : a journey from Kenya to Canada / Njoki Wane.
Names: Wane, Njoki Nathani, author.
Identifiers: Canadiana 2018903873x | ISBN 9781928088738 (softcover)
Subjects: LCSH: Wane, Njoki Nathani. | LCSH: Kenyans–Canada–Biography. | LCSH: College teachers–Canada–Biography. | LCSH: Women immigrants–Canada–Biography. | CSH: Black Canadians–Biography.
Classification: LCC FC106.B6 W466 2020 | DDC 971/.004967920092–dc23

*To Mum and Dad; Tony, Francis, Maatha,
Mike, Henry and Venancio*

May your souls rest in peace.

TABLE OF CONTENTS

FOREWORD

Many African cultures believe that we cannot know a person unless we know their roots and that no one can achieve anything of significance unless they know where "they are coming from" or "where they belong."

I know few people who are as conscious and proud of their roots as Njoki. In her memoir, she clearly shows that she's fully aware of her heritage as she fondly recounts her experiences of growing up in rural Embu. As someone who sees her on a daily basis, I have witnessed how this rootedness manifests in her many actions.

Where many Western-educated Africans (not to say Kenyans) seem to relish their "Westernization" and distance themselves from their culture, Njoki has deliberately celebrated her Kenyan and Embu beginnings. One does not have to look far for evidence of this. The fact that a young girl known "officially" as Catherine has chosen to revert to her Kenyan name of Njoki instead of the European name she had to adopt while attending Catholic school speaks volumes.

Some might misinterpret this as a rejection of European culture or norms. However, anyone who knows Njoki will see this more appropriately as evidence that one can practise what the late Senegalese writer and president Léopold Sédar Senghor advocated: "rootedness and openness." Njoki shows that one can be at the same time very attached to and respectful of one's culture while also being open and appreciative of what other cultures offer.

In this memoir Njoki shares with the reader stories about her life in Kenya and Canada. With great humour, she tells of growing up in the countryside, going to boarding school and receiving her first pair of high-heeled shoes. She also shares her life in Canada as a graduate student, then as a university professor at the University of Toronto.

There are many qualities to admire in Njoki. It will be obvious to the reader that she is a person who realizes that she has been blessed with a lot of opportunities in life and who feels it's important to share with others. Over the years, I have met many of her students who privately have told me of her many acts of kindness that went beyond what they expected of a professor.

Despite all her achievements, Njoki is a humble person who relates equally well to the very highly educated and to the rural folks she celebrates in a lot of her professional writing. I have seen her equally at ease entertaining ministers or socializing with African women farmers.

This ability to navigate between many worlds is part of what makes Njoki's memoir very entertaining and educational. Readers, irrespective of their backgrounds, will find some stories that bring a smile to their face or make them think of their own histories. Even though Njoki writes as a Kenyan, her stories will resonate with non-Kenyans and non-Africans as the themes she discusses are universal: family, school, culture. Just as she does in everyday life, Njoki makes space for everyone in her memoirs.

Amadou Wane

INTRODUCTION

It feels like just yesterday that I was a little girl hopping my way to the river to fetch water only to rush back home with an almost empty container because half the water had spilled on me. I can still remember trying to balance a small steel sufuria that my mother or my elder sisters had designated as my container for fetching water from the Ena River.

The container felt special because it was small, just like me, and my mother never used it for cooking. It was always left in the kitchen, on the wooden drying platform made of twigs, ready for me to pick it up and run to the river to fetch water. Everyone in the family knew how fast I could run (unless I was instructed otherwise) and because of that I was always the one sent for errands: buying salt or sugar from the village shops, delivering a pint of milk to my grandmother's house, being sent to the bush to look for firewood. I took great pride in my tasks even when the results weren't quite what had been expected. The only firewood small enough for me to collect was supposed to be used to make tea for my brothers' visitors. They could only laugh when I regularly returned home with a load of twigs that were not nearly dry enough to burn and could not be used for weeks, if not months!

Who cares? I thought. As long as I brought home a load of firewood, even if it could not make anybody's fire, I had fulfilled my purpose. I was imaginative and ambitious, always looking to the future and painting my world with images of wonder yet to come. I was quick to point out to my brothers or sisters that it would only be a matter of time before the world changed. That I would just press a button to prepare a cup of tea for them or turn a knob and water would flow – my imagination always carried me away. I always thought of the day when I would never have to go to the river to bring water home or go to the bushes in search of firewood.

Many times I would arrive from the river, soaking wet, and would turn to Mother and say, "Mami! When I am done with school, I will make sure you have piped water right there." I pointed to the centre of the compound. "No more calabashes or big containers on your head or back."

My mother would laugh and say, "You know, Njoki, I believe you. One day you will have water in your own home, not here: far, far from here."

All members of my family knew me as a happy little girl, very playful, full of life and nothing bothered me. I was a joyful child.

Not all my imaginings came to fruition before my mother passed on, but she was able to enjoy cooking with a gas stove and having water piped up to her compound – but not inside her house – before she died. However, she did not live to enjoy a cup of tea produced by a microwave.

Who would have thought that the small girl who used to run to Ena River to fetch water, or go to the bushes to look for firewood, would one day stand in her kitchen far from her kijiji – which means village in Kiswahili – and be pressing buttons for cooking. That she'd press a knob and water would flow, press a button and dishes would be washed.

Probably for many Canadians, my childhood seems far-fetched. It is not for someone who grew up in a small kijiji in rural Kenya. Kijiji for me was that place where everyone knew one another. Where the women assisted each other during childbirth. Where neighbours ploughed and harvested for you when you were not well. Kijiji had a sense of belonging. There was one primary school, one Protestant church, one chief. Later in the book, I talk about our evacuation during the fight for independence. People from the kijiji were forced to leave our homes; however, when independence was declared in 1963, everyone returned.

My own children did not experience my life and nor will their children. The village experience is something you might see in a movie – but that was my reality and I loved it. Today, when I look back, I experience some turmoil. There are some things I would have liked to keep from my rural life in the village, such as organic food, kinship, relationships and the spirit of the kijiji where children grew without fear. I know things like the microwave make life easier for us. However, the health impact is something I think about on a daily basis. I guess those like me who have embraced many aspects of modernity, whether in the West or in other parts of the world experience dissonance as they make sense of the complexity in their life caused by what surrounds them.

Not all lessons happen in order. Most come in fits and starts over the course of our lifetime and it is the gift of memory and our willingness to reflect that gives life and value to lessons decades in the making. How often, as an adult, have you looked back to an event in your life and thought, I see. I see now why my elders constantly repeated the same thing over and over again.

I see why they employed proverbs and riddles almost on a daily basis – particularly when there were challenges to be overcome, and especially when certain struggles did not make sense at all. Now, as I look back, I understand how these events have shaped me, made me who I am today, have made me the professor I am at the University of Toronto. When I teach, I usually challenge the students to find something from their far memory. I challenge them to recall stories they were told by their parents or their grandparents or their neighbours.

The essence of these stories is to compare our contemporary times with times from the past. My emphasis here is about one's culture or ethnicity. I find this is a good way to ground students who think they have no culture or that they are just Canadians and have no ethnic background. We are all Indigenous to a place. I say this constantly because we are all from a place; we do not have to have visited that place, but that place is carved in us. To some extent, we do connect with some of those stories from our past – and some stories are very traumatizing, while others, students remember them only as they were narrated or passed down in their family line, generation after generation. I believe sharing these stories (even if they are being told by a fifth generation) is important. They create a connective tissue, something tangible that keeps families, communities and sometimes societies together.

I believe that our most important lessons are the ones we have to wait for. Each of us has struggled, fought and despaired at some point in our lives. We may have faced down a terrifying foe or sat down at the end of the day, utterly defeated and asked ourselves, "Why me? Why do I have to fight this hard? What can I possibly learn from this much pain other than to avoid it at all costs?" Other times, we have looked back and appreciated the many blessings, the abundance in our life – and many times, we do not even think of why we have been so blessed with so much. It does not make sense.

Let me give you an example: Even when I was eight years old, I wanted to be a professor. Do you know how long I waited for that to happen? It was not a straight path. For instance, I waited for almost seven years to join university. Why? Why could I not go from high school to university like all my classmates? Why did my mother die before I graduated? Or, why did I have so much material wealth in my early twenties when I could not make sense of it, while some girls of my age had little to nothing, and then have next to nothing in my thirties? Life is extremely complex and many of us go through it not noticing what is happening. There is too much of the unevenness of abundance.

But for me, as I sit to reflect on my journey, I believe my experiences have been so beautiful, so rich that I would not have wanted my life to have unfolded differently. I have enjoyed the simple things in life. I have enjoyed grand aspects of life. I also have enjoyed counting pennies because I did not have enough money to feed my Canadian family, and later in life, when I finally got my teaching job, I enjoyed treating them to good dinners and outings. These are the moments that shape us; these are the memories that carve our future from the woodwork of possibility. Struggle and challenge, appreciation and gratitude narrow our focus, define our values and provide us with stillness necessary for grounding. *From My Mother's Back* is a story told through lessons and connections, pairing the present with the past to allow the reader to experience the complete phenomenon of what it means to have a meaningful life full of abundance. I believe the present is a mirror of my past. The struggles made me strong, made me appreciate my parents' teachings. The constant use of proverbs would be a reminder that even the difficult moments will soon pass: *no matter how long the night, dawn will come.* Looking back, I have been blessed with great family members; the good in my life outweighs the challenges.

This story is about real-life events and will explore many issues, including culture, spirituality, education and status, as well as personal drive, family values and the fickle nature of destiny.

Gratitude shapes a person as often as grief and this story is filled with all the necessary ingredients to grow a strong, independent and thoughtful woman or man. You will see mistakes, judgment and selfish pride as often as you see strength, integrity and humility. I encourage you to react to each story as it comes rather than wait to see what happens next.

So often in life, we are offered only a brief snapshot of an individual's character and we must make decisions based on that single interaction, observation or event. Only with the people we spend most of our time with do we have the luxury of watching an individual grow, struggle and adapt.

And even then, we miss most of what truly makes them who they are: reflection, self-evaluation – a resolution to change when necessary. More often than not, such a process happens in the privacy and sanctity of our own minds, rarely shared and even more rarely dissected in depth.

Each of these chapters has a story to tell. Each one of them narrates a memorable moment or event. Respond to each chapter; judge each person as if you will never meet them again. Only then will you be able to truly connect with the emotional, spiritual and mental minefield that makes a person who they are; what makes me the person I am today.

Remember, it is often a twist of fate whether or not we meet a person on their best day, their worst or in the midst of growth. Some say that people never really change. This could not be more false. People change all the time, on a minute-by-minute or even second-by-second basis, sometimes in such extreme ways that they appear to be completely different people. These changes are not discarded; rather they are experienced, evaluated and adjusted faster than most people can imagine.

Change is part of human instinct. We adapt to every situation as best we can, learning what works, throwing away what doesn't. As a resident of Canada and a citizen, I have adapted to many things that I would never have imagined. For instance, I do appreciate the four seasons of the year, though I grew up in a climate that was constant and was marked by rainy or dry seasons, or by ploughing, planting, weeding and harvesting seasons. There is beauty when you take in every breath in the surroundings that you consider home even in its impermanence. I talk about this temporary feeling because once a person lives in different continents, it is difficult to completely consider one place more permanent than the other one. When I am in Kenya, I constantly talk about my home in Canada. And, when I am in Canada, I always talk about my home in Kenya. So, where is home for me?

Of course I have also had many encounters in both countries when people would ask me, "When will you go back?" Perhaps think of me as if I was suspended in the air, casting my gaze in both directions, northwest to Canada and southeast to Kenya. Or those times when someone would ask me, "Where are you really from?" This is a very common question in the West especially when you are not of Caucasian background. When I respond with "Pickering," they insist on their interpretation and say, "No – you cannot be. You speak with an accent." If I have some time to engage in a dialogue, I often ask my questioner, "Where are you from yourself?" They answer, of course, Canada. I then respond, "That is good – it's always great to meet an Indigenous person from Turtle Island." And the conversation would shift somehow and my questioner would say – "Oh, oh – I am not an Aboriginal person. My ancestors came from ..." and they would name the country.

These conversations are always a reminder to me that I am in transit; I really do not have a permanent home. These are the moments that I feel homesick, that I experience a sense of alienation and dislocation, and feel a lack of belonging. And, at the same time, a sense of gratitude. Gratitude for the opportunity to have my spirit floating in different continents in search of home, in search of beauty, in search of something that has no name, yes something – though I'm not sure what.

Consider, therefore, the lessons in this book and decide for yourself what should be remembered, what should be changed and what should be forgotten.

Fulfillment of a Prophecy: A University Professor

My mother can see this; I am certain of it.

This is what she always wanted for me: a life of academics rather than field work. I can feel her eyes upon me, full of love and pride: a pride that once embarrassed me, a pride I once rejected. This rejection was the mistake of a young and selfish child: one that I will never make again. It has been a long journey from the Ena River in rural Kenya where, at the tender age of eight years, I insisted to my dearest friend Patricia that someday I was going to be a professor speaking to an auditorium full of students in a university. Were my words to Patricia a fantasy? A prophecy? A dream – the product of some wild imagination evoked in children's play? It seemed so at the time. Yet, today, I am not only a professor, but one who has received a number of teaching awards, the most recent one being the President's Teaching Award from the University of Toronto.

I will not lie to you; as I write these lines, I am blinking away tears. It is extremely emotional for me to consider the long road that I have travelled – physically, emotionally, spiritually and professionally – to be where I am today. What makes me shed tears when I look back is how supportive many people have been. Believe you me, I have met strangers who have assisted in more ways than one can imagine.

I still remember one such incident when a stranger gave me forms to apply for a scholarship to Canadian universities. This is how I found myself at the University of New Brunswick in Fredericton to pursue a master's degree in education. Another time, a mentor whom I had not seen for about five years rang the gate bell of my Nairobi home because she was lost. When I opened the gate, she said, "Oh my, you were the last person I expected to see in this neighbourhood" (this will make sense to you later). Not making sense of what she meant, I invited her in, but she declined as she was looking for a friend's house, who happened to be my next-door neighbour. However, before she left, she asked me casually whether I would be interested in teaching for her – she was a deputy principal of Kianda College – for one semester as their regular teacher was on maternity leave. Without hesitation, I said yes. I did not have a college diploma, nor a teaching certificate. All I had were a few secretarial certificates that I had acquired from that college a few years back. That was the beginning of my teaching career. One semester became one year. In the space of that year, my life changed completely.

I still remember Mrs. Wamokoya, a colleague at Kianda College, who approached me a few days before the end of the academic year and gave me a newspaper cutting advertising a one-year teacher training program for business education teachers. I looked at her, not sure why she gave it to me, and I said, "I am not interested in joining anybody's teachers' college. I am satisfied teaching a few hours a day and going home to rest. I actually don't need the money as a full-time employee. My life is okay."

I will never forget the look this woman gave me. Then she proceeded to say, "You are a real fool. What's wrong with you? Open your eyes to reality and get something for yourself. Do not depend on other people's money." I felt insulted and left the staff room. When I came back, she handed me a handwritten note. It was an application letter responding to the advertisement for the one-year teacher training program with my name on it. Without waiting for me to say a word she said, "Sign here." I signed the letter without even reading it, and left the room again.

On reflection, I am not sure why I signed that letter. One thing, however, is clear: that signature put me back on track on my educational journey. Maybe I signed the letter out of respect for her, as I had been taught to be respectful. I did not care whether I got admitted to the college or not. I was more concerned with what the principal of the Kianda College would say if she knew I was planning to leave for a teacher training program. However, on reflection, it was the unconscious dream in me to be a professor that guided me. Mrs. Wamokoya was my angel. She was one of the many guides that I have met throughout my life.

Call it fate. But someone had to intervene to save me from my folly. Mrs. Wamokoya was a trained teacher, she was mature, and she could read my naïveté from a mile away. I was in my early twenties, and I never thought that one day, I would wake up from my dream (honestly, I was living a good life: fantasy cars, big homes, vacationing in Europe, flying first class) with no money or cars, nothing except my diplomas. My life was extremely good – or so I thought.

A month later, I received an invitation for an interview for the training program. I was scared. I did not know how to excuse myself for the day. I turned to Mrs. Wamokoya and asked her what I should say to the principal. I still remember her words: "Oh my goodness, what's wrong with you? This is your life. Tell the principal you have business to take care of." This time, she walked out of the staff room and left me there gazing into nothingness. I cannot remember what excuse I gave the principal for being absent; what I remember is how scared I was to walk to the principal's office to ask for a day off work.

What I remember vividly is driving to Kenya Technical Teachers College for my interview. I walked into the interview room with pride and confidence. I had already made up my mind that this interview was a waste of my time and I couldn't wait to be done with it. I still remember telling the panellist that my dream was to attend a university and become a professor and that what the college offered me would not be enough to equip me with the education I was searching for. Interestingly, one of the panellists was a Canadian professor. Nevertheless, despite my attitude, I passed the interview and within a month, I was sitting in a classroom as a trainee at the Kenya Technical Teachers College in Nairobi. My long road to the acquisition of many degrees had just begun. Mrs. Wamokoya was my angel. She snapped me from sleep and put me back on my path to becoming a university professor. The ground had shifted beneath me. My view of the material world completely changed. All that I longed for now was to achieve my mother's dream for me – to acquire a university degree. I have had many such incidences, especially in Canada.

My one-year diploma training at the Kenya Technical Teachers College was one of my best times in life. I excelled in all my subjects. I met women who became my lifelong family friends. Through my honours diploma, I was admitted to Nairobi University, Kenyatta College Campus to pursue my bachelor of education in business studies.

I have met many such angels as Mrs. Wamokoya both in Canada and Kenya, people who have directed me in one way or another. My mum who was already in the spirit world kept me company all the time. And now, as I write this memoir, I have many members of my family who walk with me as they also have transitioned to the spirit world: people whom I cannot touch, or hear their voice or have them hear mine as I narrate my stories – I do miss them, my parents, my brothers and Mike, the father of some of my children.

Mum, you started this journey with me, I know you can see me. Please come, as I want us to remember my first experience as a professor in a Canadian university. I had taught previously in a Kenyan university, but without a master's degree – again one of those occurrences in my life where strangers guided me as I tried to move away from my path. Mum – walk beside me – here I am, walking into the auditorium for my first class of the fall semester.

The walk from my car to the classroom is filled with an unfamiliar excitement. I've walked, driven, flown and sailed to many new places. I've been full of wonder seeing Niagara Falls in Canada, the foothills of Mount Kenya, the Taj Mahal on the south bank of the Yamuna River in the Indian city of Agra, the slave castles in Senegal and many others, but this is the first time I am going somewhere where I am both extremely nervous and excited all at once.

"Mama, we have taken this path together many times when I was a child. It never matters whether it's concrete or loose soil. I walk beside you, Mother. I learn from you and I teach from you."

I whisper these words to myself as I pull my carrying case behind me, knowing that my ancestors are listening. Conversations with spirits are something I learned from my father. He received much guidance from them and today, I do as well.

The University of Toronto campus is beautiful, full of life and bursting with potential. I look around and pause a moment to take in the beauty of these magnificent-looking buildings built in the eighteenth century, and I sigh. The concrete walkways, grassy quads and towering buildings remind me of how far I am from my village (fourteen thousand kilometres), and yet, how close to home. Seasons are still something at which I marvel. The golden leaves of fall, crisp winter snow and fresh winds of spring are all gifts of this new country. But then, momentarily, I am taken back to Kenya.

Kenya is a land of diversity: from the mountains where my village is to the arid areas of North Eastern province, the white sandy beaches of Coastal province or the tea farms in the Rift Valley. I always breathe deeply while travelling through those areas, taking in the contrast of the landscape of my country. Yet, we had nothing like Canadian winters where the world comes to a standstill, grounds covered in a white carpet with tree branches draped with crystals. There's a longing that comes with it – to be back home – back in my kijiji sitting in the courtyard with my brothers, listening to Dad's stories of his conversations with spirits and passing along his traditional teaching.

Strangely, the cold Canadian winters remind me of the warm sunny Kenyan days. No matter how many years I spend here, it will always feel a bit foreign, like being on vacation. Whenever I fly home to Kenya, I wrap myself in its familiarity: the laughter of children walking to or from school all by themselves; the people shaking hands with a particular kind of feeling of *I know you, I see you, I feel you*; the relationships, how people relate to me; the surroundings, the trees, the food and, most enjoyably, the mothering warmth of the African rhythms. Some might prefer drastic changing seasons, but I live for the African rhythms. Canada has been home for me for many years now, a home away from home. I am a woman of two worlds and I am not the only one.

The heavy doors swing open before me as I make my way down the echoing hallway to the auditorium where I am going to teach a second-year class. I take care to avoid distracted students as they walk in the meandering lines marked with course corrections prompted by near misses with pillars, walls, doors, trash cans and water fountains.

Cell phones have become essential navigation tools to this generation and yet I can't help but notice that, though they plan their lives in the palm of their hands, planning to walk a straight line down the hallway in school seems to be an insurmountable task. Perhaps they'll "update" soon.

My children recently convinced me to purchase a new cell phone. A smart phone, they said. The new phone is good, but I use maybe a quarter of the features it offers. My children are constantly making fun of me. They, like many of these students, prefer to have access to everyone all the time.

"I remember a time," I tell them, "when someone would actually have to write out a letter and mail it to their loved ones."

They laugh and tease me.

"Mama! That was a long time ago. Besides, why would you want to waste all that time writing out a letter when you can just send a text, or Instagram? This makes much more sense, you'll see."

I smile as I see glimmers of my daughters and sons in each student that I pass. No matter where we are from, it seems that technology brings us all together.

My bags are getting heavy and I wonder how the students would react if I hoisted my packages and balanced them on my head for the remainder of the journey?

Perhaps I'll save that one for later; I'm nearly to the correct auditorium anyway.

I prefer to get to my appointments early so it is no surprise to me when I enter the vast lecture hall and there are only a handful of students sitting in the stadium-style seats. Some are typing away on their laptops while others are writing or doodling on their paper tablets. The breadth of technology always makes me smile and I wonder how long it will take before they all turn into audio recorders.

Their quiet chatter reminds me of a time when I sat in a classroom, waiting for the bell to ring. Their laughter warms me. I like to think that some of them, hopefully all of them, are enjoying their education. Learning is such a privilege, but so many experience it as a burden. I hope that my class will be a place where the burden is lifted.

Rather than go to the front of the room, I decide to sit and observe for a moment. I take a seat in the front row turning my body to the side so I can see the students all around me. I sit directly in front of the lectern from where I will later teach the class. Students tend to change their behaviour when the professor enters the room and I am curious to see my pupils in action before they start "behaving themselves."

I feel like an anthropologist observing a mysterious culture in their "native habitat." In all honesty, I shouldn't be too difficult to spot as the professor but it is my first day of teaching as a full faculty member and I want to appreciate the moment.

As the start time draws closer, more students begin to filter in, some in a hurry to sit with their friends while others shuffle in with their heads down and find a seat in an unoccupied section. I can't help but wonder which works better? Do you sit with your friends in comfort or by yourself in academic solitude? I know my preference, but I wonder if that extends to others.

With the arrival of more students comes more noise and soon the auditorium is filled with the buzz of nearly two hundred students carrying as many conversations. It still amazes me how they can switch from topic to topic and person to person without getting lost or forgetting what was being said in the first place.

Do they take notes? Perhaps that's what their phones are really for.

I listen for a moment and hear everything from updates on sporting events, social gatherings yet to be scheduled, memories from summer break to classes attended earlier in the day.

Will they talk about my class after the bell rings and they leave for the day?

Will they reflect and question?

What will they say to their peers about Professor Wane's class?

I hope they are as conscientious about their assignments, but I know better than to count on it.

Some look so serious while others look completely uninterested and still others appear to be attending a weekend social. I wonder why some of them bother to show up at all as they appear to be miserable or barely awake; this is an elective course, after all. I suppose I'll find out as the semester wears on and I've learned my lesson about associating a student's apparent enthusiasm with their work ethic. The two are barely related.

One young lady turns to me quite suddenly and smiles brightly before introducing herself.

"Hey, I'm Linda. Do you know anything about this professor? Is he hard? Do you think there will be a lot of work?"

I chuckle.

He? Interesting.

"I'm sorry," I reply. "I don't know anything about *him*."

I doubt my emphasis on *him* means much to her and since she didn't ask me for my name, I feel no obligation to offer one. Apparently, my lack of knowledge means our conversation is over and Linda turns away from me and back to her friends, probably to speculate further on how difficult the course will be and just who this Njoki Wane might be.

The start time for the course comes and goes and I decide to wait a bit to see what they're going to do. No one has made an effort to turn their attention to the front of the class and I wonder if they've noticed the time at all.

While I know there are some students on campus that have returned to school after a career and are older than the average student, there aren't that many of them and I find it fascinating that not one student in this two-hundred-person lecture hall has thought I might be the professor they're all waiting for.

How odd.

I'll wonder more about that later.

After observing for five more minutes, I stand up and make my way to the front of the auditorium. At first, no one notices and the chatter continues as I arrange my books and notes on the side table.

Eventually, I decide that my little experiment is over. Now is the time to make myself known. I'm sure it will come as quite a surprise to Linda and her friends and I am curious to see their reactions. I walk to the lectern and deftly flick the microphone switch to the "on" position. However, before I say anything, I write my full name on the board, followed by "Who can read this for us?"

After some students shout different pronunciations of my name, I take the microphone and say: "Hello, ladies and gentlemen. I am your professor for this course, Dr. Njoki Nathani Wane. Welcome to your first lecture. I hope you've all found the syllabus and have the required reading list. Before we begin, I would like to point out to you the correct pronunciation of my name. This room is made up of people from different backgrounds, cultures and languages. This is a space where I will learn from you and you will learn from me . . . we shall learn from each other."

The hush that rushes over the room makes me chuckle once more and I spare a quick glance in Linda's direction. She's pressed back into her chair, back straight and eyes wide open. I smile at her, assuring her that my ruse was not a joke at her expense before continuing with my introduction.

"This course is not about turning in papers, answering questions correctly or memorizing facts. In fact, I would prefer you didn't."

The looks on their faces remind me of my own experience as an undergraduate student.

"This course is about learning to pay attention to things we would normally overlook, asking questions that we would normally not bother with and seeking facts that might otherwise go unnoticed.

"I urge you to prepare for hard work, but perhaps not in the sense that you are used to. It is my hope that, by the end of this course, you will never look at your peers, your family or even strangers the same way again. However, before we start, I would like to tell you about myself, my research, my education ..."

For the next ten minutes I let the students know how I came to be in that class, how I earned my position and what it takes to be a professor. As I look around at the students' faces, I can tell my performance seems to have paid off. There is silence in class where there was only the din of chatter and social media minutes before. Many students are staring at me.

"Was that necessary, Njoki?"

I hear my mother's voice.

"Yes, I want the world to know I am a learned woman; a proud daughter of Africa and your child."

Later, after the students having filed out and empty silence has once more descended in the room, however briefly, I savour this day. Introducing myself to this room, standing before them as a professor at this university, presenting myself to two hundred students, all there to learn something from me, is one of the proudest moments of my life. I wish my parents were alive to witness this moment.

I choke with tears as I look up to salute them because I know they are in the room, although in spirit. I know they can hear me and I know they were present today. I smile at the thought of their being here, standing next to me, guiding me as they always have and relishing the emergence of reality, a reality that was once nothing more tangible than a child's fantasy in an empty field . . .

Saying my name out loud, announcing myself as a professor of this university, echoes through my mind and I cannot help but indulge myself one more time. There are a few minutes left before the next class begins to wander in.

I stand behind the lectern and say, "My name is Professor Njoki Wane. This is my class, you are my students and I will teach you something you've never heard before."

I smile hearing the raw honesty in my own voice. Every word is true and I know what a gift that is. I recall another moment in my life when I introduced myself as Njoki and rather than accept that name, a different one was demanded of me, a name I did not have, a name from other traditions. Today I am strong enough to decline, offer my true name or none at all, but I was not always so strong, so proud of who I was and where I came from.

Enchantment of Enrolling in Primary School

A boarding school!

I was going to sign up for a new school today!

Far, far from my village and I could hardly sit still. My neighbours' father had agreed to take four girls from the village, me included, for an interview to this faraway school. My imagination was driving me crazy. I visualized all kinds of things: I could see myself walking in the hallways, playing hide and seek, chasing butterflies in the schoolyard ... Oh! I could not wait to see this school.

I could not believe how wonderful this was going to be! What was I going to learn? Who was I going to meet? Where would I live?

The sheer number of questions threatened to overwhelm me as I sat quietly in the back seat and we drove down on the dusty winding road toward the Sacred Heart Girls School, a Catholic boarding school run by Italian nuns for girls only. I didn't really know what *Catholic* meant, but I was sure it was just lovely. I thought about how I looked back and saw Mother standing in the road watching the car disappear and some sadness gripped me. If I got admitted to this school, what would happen to our walks to the farm? Who would narrate stories from the novels for her?

What about my friend Patricia? Who would walk with her to the river? Who would assist Njeru (my younger brother) to look after the goats or cows? Who would play with him? What would happen to our weekly swim in Ena River with my young nephews and Njeru? Was I abandoning my mother, my friends, my brother? Why could I not continue in the same school as my sister Emily and with all my other friends? Why was my sister Wanyiri insisting that I go to this school?

The ride was as comfortable as it was rare. Come to think of it, this was the first time I had ridden in my neighbour's car. This was my first time in a car – I had been in a bus, but not a car – it was an experience I will never forget. The joy of riding in one car, as a family, brothers and sisters, their mom and dad. Why couldn't my dad own a car? Well, one day, I thought to myself, I will own a car, and I will drive my children and my mom all over my village. I thought it was really cool. I couldn't imagine how I would have ever gotten to the school walking from home. The place was *far*. Wambere's dad did not make one stop to let us use the bathroom, not even for five minutes. Is that what it means to ride in cars? I thought. That you're not allowed to stop until you get to where you're going? If I was walking with Mother, I would have told her and she would have stopped and waited for me to empty my bladder . . . I thought of my mum, she was far from here. She was so happy that I was learning more than what we had found in my books though I could see the sadness in her eyes that she tried to hide as the car drove off.

Would Mama miss me? Would I miss her?

The walks to the farm were long, but I did not want to trade in my excitement to read or dip my feet in the stream at the bottom of our small coffee farm for going to a far-away school. I wondered if she would miss having me in the fields reading to her on our lunch breaks. I wasn't going to be away forever, though. I would be home during the holidays and I would be sure to tell her every little thing I had learnt while I was away. I would remember everything for her and then I would tell it all again to Patricia. I'm sure she would love to hear about all my adventures and per-haps one day, she would come to this school with me too. What fun that would be!

The winding road seemed endless, but my excitement didn't waver. Eventually, I saw a small building in the dis-tance and thought, This must be it!

My brother Anthony and sister Wanyiri had given me clear instructions on how to behave once I got to this place. Wanyiri knew the school fairly well, having attended it with our sister, Judy. I needed to concentrate because I did not want to make a single mistake. I hoped I had brought every-thing I needed: pencil, eraser?

Surely, all I need is me?

As we got closer, the building seemed to grow as if it was a giant tree springing from the earth. What I had originally thought to be a small building was transforming before my eyes into a monstrous, dark and imposing thing. I had no words to describe what I saw. Not even in the great markets had I seen a structure so large.

How are we supposed to get inside? I wondered. Are we even supposed to go inside?

I took a look at my bare feet, my little dress, and all of a sudden, I felt shy – I looked at the other children that we came with, they seemed confident, and all were wearing nice clothes and shoes.

Perhaps it would be best to stay outside while they go in? No. I would follow them inside. Otherwise, I would have no story for Mother or my friend Patricia or my brother Njeru. I almost missed a step as I stared at this giant *box*, examining its every detail. The stones were rough and looked nothing like bricks made from the soil that made our home. These were as dark as a wet stone. I wondered if they were as cold as they seemed to be, though I can't believe anything is as cold as the waters of Ena River.

There was a wide, two-level staircase that led to the school entrance. The archway provided steps that were very inviting and I was suddenly moved to sit and stare at this magnificent building. I trotted up the stairs and followed the other girls, completely forgetting my earlier worry over my bare feet. There were other young girls, some my age and some a bit older, milling around the tables that had been placed just outside the entrance.

As I stepped into the building, I felt an enormous weight on my shoulders. Everyone seemed absorbed in whatever they were doing and few were smiling. Allowing myself a moment to observe the activity at the tables, I took another step forward ... forward to the world of the unknown ... forward to sign up for *school*.

Wonderful!

I had made it. My mother and father would be pleased that I had made the journey without going off course or getting distracted. Normally, their concern would have been warranted but my excitement to complete this task far outweighed the temptation to ask other girls to play with me. Besides, I wasn't going to start school right away so I could play with them later.

I stepped in line behind Rafiki, one of the three girls who had also received a ride from our neighbour. All the girls who came for the interview with their parents were dressed differently from me. I recognized the adults' style of clothes as similar to what my father wore. He preferred suits and ties and polished black shoes, unlike my mother who wore a simple dress from the Indian Stores and no shoes at all. Sometimes, she wore flip-flops but most of the time, she was barefoot like me ... I liked that. Of course, for Father, now a retired government officer, it would make sense that he dressed the way a government man would.

I wondered where all these people that filled the room were from. Did they live in the city or were they from a village like me? Did they take a car or did they walk?

I glanced down at people's feet and quickly decided I was the only odd one out ... no shoes. Were we supposed to have shoes at school? I didn't have shoes. I only had my slippers. Did that matter? Would someone be upset with me?

My mind raced with questions and panic gripped my chest. Just as I was about to step out of line, for fear that they would throw me out for my lack of shoes, Rafiki turned to me, having completed filling the forms, and stepped aside for me to move ahead.

It was my turn.

There was a young woman sitting before me, dressed in a long white robe and a funny white scarf covering every bit of her hair. Her skin was pale, as were her eyes, and I wondered if the sun ever bothered her. She stared at me for a moment as I stared at her, before placing her pen on the table and waving her hand at a similarly dressed woman. Why did the woman look so different? I wondered what might have happened to her skin? Before I could start feeling sorry for her condition, the second pale woman joined us and she said to me, in Kiembu, my mother tongue, "What is your name?"

Her voice was stern and slightly impatient. Had I already done something wrong? I was just feeling bad for them, because of their skin condition. Who were they and where did they come from? Why was she so angry with me? This wasn't how things were supposed to go! The panic tightening my chest increased and I struggled to remember my earlier excitement. After more than one deep breath and a couple of false starts, I managed to say, "My name is Njoki."

The two women were clearly not pleased with my answer and I struggled to find another one. My quest was quick and fruitless. Njoki is my name, there's no doubt about that and no other answer for their question that I knew.

"No, no!" she said, facial expression unchanged but voice becoming more agitated. How did she do that? Shouldn't her face change if she was getting angry?

"Njoki is not a name. What is your Christian name? Your given name?"

"My Christian name?" I asked. "What is a Christian name?"

"Is your name Mary or Sarah or Catherine?"

Catherine?

That sounds lovely!

"My name is Catherine," I announced, pleased to have chosen a name so beautiful and exotic.

"Very well," the seated woman stated. "Catherine with a C or a K?"

Oh no! Another choice. C or K? C sounds even more exotic.

"Catherine with a C," I stated firmly.

"Fine, you can now join the other girls and write your test. Your results will be sent to your home or your father can come and find out if you have been successful."

I stared, unmoving as she shuffled some papers together.

"Okay, Catherine; take these papers back to your parents."

Mutely, I accepted the offered documents and rubbed the paper between my fingers. What had I just done?

"Catherine, I am talking to you..."

It took two or three minutes to register – the woman at the desk was talking to me! I turned around and took the papers without even looking at them.

This was the first time that I had seen people who did not look like me or my friends. I wasn't sure why they were wearing white headscarves and long white dresses. Was this going to be our uniform as well? And why were they being called "sisters?" Were they all related like me and my sisters? Did they not have names? Why did these women insist on calling me by another name? At the moment, I decided not to say anything to my parents and wait for the results of the interview. After all, if I didn't pass the test, maybe they would never know. My heart was still racing and I let out an ecstatic giggle as I realized that I had actually managed to enroll myself in school. And, it was going to start in less than two months! Oh, I was so excited. Not even the confusing environment could change that.

I went over my conversation with the woman in my head on the ride home. I didn't want to forget anything. I wanted to share my adventure with Njeru and Patricia.

When I returned home, I announced proudly to my parents: "Mother, Father, I have had an interview and if I pass, I will be gone for some time! I will be attending this big, big school, built with only stones and our teachers will be pale-looking women all dressed in white and they cover their heads with scarves. Yes, in less than two months..."

My brothers laughed at my enthusiasm, my mother smiled and my father nodded his head. After my announcement, we began our evening meal since they had waited for me to return from my interview. It was a full week later that I realized I had forgotten to give them the papers.

I did not know at the time of my registration in the school that the name Catherine would become part of my identity, haunting me as I tried to drop it or explain its origin later in life.

I recall quickly when my brother Anthony came through the door one week later, anger in his eyes and announced to my father, "Njoki lied! She did not enroll in school. She did not even do the interview! I went today to check and her name was not on the list!"

My father turned to me and I shrank at the look on his face. I didn't dare look at my mother because, while my father led the family, my mother was the disciplinarian and if I didn't explain quickly, it was going to be her delivering my punishment.

"No!" I cried. "I did the interview. My name is on their books. I have the papers."

I rushed into the room I shared with my mother and brother Njeru and fetched the papers I had tucked away. Handing them over to my father, I waited silently for the verdict. After a moment he asked, "Who is Catherine Njoki?"

I didn't understand the question.

"Baba, when the woman asked my name, I told her I was Njoki and she said I was wrong. Then she asked what my Christian name was and said it was either Mary, Sarah or Catherine. I chose Catherine with a C because it's so pretty and then they said I was done. I'm sorry I forgot to give you the papers."

I'm still not sure what my father thought of the whole situation, but my brothers started laughing loudly and at length. Not even my mother could stop a few chuckles from escaping. In one month's time, I would begin my first term as Catherine Njoki and I couldn't be more excited.

This letter marked the end of my traditional teachings and the beginning of my indoctrination into a foreign way of living, spiritual practices and education, different culture and morning rituals. What was unfortunate for me was that my parents did not know that my traditional teachings were not going to be taken up in the new school. They trusted the sisters wholeheartedly to prepare their daughter to be who she wanted to be. My parents did not know that the sisters' teaching, their way of life, had no space for ours. My African teachings would be squashed and pushed to a distant memory, but not completely lost. I say this with pride, because many years later I picked up the threads that I had dropped at the entrance of my primary education and started on a quest to research, teach and write on African Indigenous knowledges and in particular, education and spirituality.

Office Hours

Office hours for professors are often a test of preparedness; you never know who's going to walk through your door – if anyone walks through at all – and you never really know what they're going to need from you. One thing you can always be certain of: whatever they want, they're going to want it right now.

Being a professor of Sociology and Equity Studies often means students come to me for interpreting, clarifying or resolving personal experiences. While such a role would typically be reserved for a family member, some students find surrogates in their professors and reach out with far more than typical academic questions.

My office hours have long been a source of adventure and creative demand that rivals a television drama. Whether it is questions about homesickness, identity or spiritual con-fusion, topics for their thesis or theoretical frameworks, the final term paper score or experiences with racism, or any other form of discrimination, office hours require the undi-vided attention of my heart and mind. On rare occasions, students actually come to discuss something from the class that day. Such visits always bring with them a small sense of reward because I get first-hand confirmation that the student is listening and thinking about what I teach.

So, after a lecture on family and ancestral origin, I am pleasantly surprised to find a young lady, Anna is her name, standing outside my office with a contemplative look on her face. As she becomes aware of my approach, she straight-ens from her slouch against the wall, shifts her books to one hand and smiles. I can't help but notice that, despite her smile, she seems troubled and I mentally prepare my-self to switch from professor to counsellor as I cross the threshold and invite her in.

"Good afternoon, Anna. What brings you here today?"

I know better than to ask, "What's the problem?" since the question tends to provoke problem-based conversations.

"Good afternoon, Professor. I have a question for you."

"Wonderful," I reply. "I love questions. What caught your attention?"

She takes a moment to collect her thoughts and I realize that this topic might be a bit difficult for Anna to broach. I quickly review our lecture topic, trying to identify any elements that might provoke such turmoil. Nothing immediately stands out, which leads me to believe that her question is of a more personal nature than an academic or philosophical one.

After all my years of teaching, I have yet to develop a clear way to predict what parts of my lectures will trigger personal vs. academic controversy. Each student's experience is so unique that sometimes the simplest statement can be as evocative as a statement left unmade. I've had as many questions about why I *didn't* mention something as why I did. They get me every time . . . and I love it. My students keep me humble and forever learning.

"When you were talking about family and ancestors, I guess I just don't see what the big deal is."

For someone who "doesn't see what the big deal is," she sure seems to be quickly building on some emotion. Anna shifts in her seat. Her eyes touch every surface in my office but never land on me. I wonder if she's worried about offending me.

"Of course," I say, trying to open the door a bit wider for this conversation. "Each person places a different value on family and where they came from. My interpretation will be different from yours. It only makes sense that it be so. Now, tell me, what did my lecture mean to you?"

Giving her the space to disagree with me and still be "right" seems to bolster her resolve and Anna dives into the meat of the issue.

"Okay, I was born and raised in Canada. My parents and I moved to a couple of different cities growing up but for the majority, I've been in the same place all my life. I consider myself Canadian. My parents consider themselves Canadian.

"Today, you said something about how we can't really know who we are without knowing where we came from … and I know that you mean more than our previous address. But, I don't really see why that is. I know who I am, and as far as I'm concerned, I come from Canada. My grandparents are from Brazil, but they died when I was really young. I've never been to Brazil. I don't know anything about it and I don't really see why I should. Brazil is not a part of my life.

"But, according to you, I can't know who I am until I know Brazil, Brazilian culture and the part of my family that is from there. My mixed ancestry … yes, African, Aboriginal, Indian from India and Scottish. Who am I, Professor? Which part of me should I leave out? For instance, I know nothing about Africa, although many times when I meet people, they always ask me which country in Africa do I come from? And, of course, I tell them, I am Canadian; however, they are quick to insist, 'But you are not white. You must be from somewhere. Where are you really from?' I just don't get it, and then your lecture; I really got frustrated and confused and I do not agree with your arguments."

What a brave girl! I can remember only a handful of times in my life when I had the courage to disagree with my professors, and certainly not at her age. She is only a twenty-two-year-old, first-year master of arts degree student. This is good, I tell myself. The best way to learn is to at first disagree. It is so much better to struggle with new information than to accept it blindly.

"Good for you, Anna!"

I see that my compliment shocks her, but I push on, not wanting to waste this opportunity.

"You disagree. That is a good place to start. I thank you for putting in the effort to truly consider my words. Now, if you are willing, I would like to try a little experiment."

Anna nods, seeming to become more comfortable with our conversation.

"Tell me a story about dinner with your family."

She laughs out loud and I am relieved to see her mood lighten. This does not have to be painful.

"Okay, um . . . let's see. Last time I had a home-cooked meal with my parents was for my birthday."

She smiles at the memory. Her eyes become distant and her voice, pleasant and warm. I imagine that this is the feeling she gets when she walks through the door of her parents' house.

"Dinner is usually a big deal. We invite friends and any family that's in the area. Dinner is supposed to be at 6:00 p.m., but it never really starts until 7:00 or 7:30. Mom cooks whatever she feels like; I'm sure some of the recipes are pretty old. I guess some of them might be from Brazil or Africa or India or . . . I don't know. We talk and laugh and there's always some outrageous story and lots of jokes. And eventually, when everyone starts to head home, we say goodbyes. I give everyone three kisses and it usually takes about half an hour or an hour to get everyone out the door."

"What a lovely event!" I say. "Such a rich experience."

"I guess so. I know some of my friends have family dinners that are kinda like that, but they just don't invite over as many people."

"I see, I see. Now, may I ask a question?"

"Sure," Anna says, now openly curious.

"Why three kisses?"

Anna stalls. She looks completely confused.

"Oh, I . . . uh. I don't really know."

"Would you be willing to complete a little homework assignment for me?"

"Of course. Now I just want to know where you're going with this."

"Perhaps, in the time between today and our next lecture, you might find out why you kiss three times?"

Anna leaves my office shortly after that and I can only hope that she follows through with the voluntary assignment.

Two days later, I have another lecture with Anna's class and, sure enough, when I get back to my office she is there, leaning against the wall. But this time, instead of a look of contemplation, she has a little smirk that makes me laugh out loud.

"It's a Brazilian thing," she says. "Single women kiss three times. Married women kiss twice. I had no idea. I was just doing what I'd seen my family members do."

We walk inside and Anna tells me more about what she's learned. Apparently, she has a number of little "habits" that she thought were random choices. Her interest in Brazil and its culture is beginning to blossom and I see her changing as well. She is more curious, not just about her own culture, but the cultures of others as well.

Anna is comparing and contrasting customs, listening to phrasing and observing gestures, and is always a student of her environment. Before she leaves my office, Anna says, "Professor, I found my keys. I just have to find the right locks. Is that what you said in class? You remember when we read that article by Two Trees about finding your keys? I think I have found them. Thank you, Prof. See you next week."

I love this feeling of teaching and being taught at the same time. I am reminded that not everyone knows where they come from. Not everyone has the information and experience readily available. And, I am more certain than ever that it is essential to know where we come from, so we know where we might go next. I make a note to myself to include Amilcar Cabral's book *Return to the Source* (1973) in next year's reading list. Out loud I say, "I am still my mother's child, always thinking about my African roots."

Reading through a Daughter's Eyes: In the Fields with My Mother

The road to our farmland is long from our home. We have to walk for almost an hour to get to our fields. We grow coffee, yams, arrowroots and fruits that my father introduced to our community from his travels. I'm not quite sure where he got the seeds from or who taught him all the things he knows as both a Veterinary Officer and an Agricultural Officer. I can still remember my visits to Mwea, the faraway town where he was in charge of the veterinary department. I'll not complain about sweet grapefruits or lemons or guavas.

Oh, I can still remember my first trip with my mother and my brother Njeru when we visited my dad. I can still see myself running away when I saw a passenger truck for the first time. How could something that had no head, eyes or legs move and what made it worse was the fact that Mother wanted me to enter this boxlike thing. I can still remember the people running after me as I ran toward our village. I did not want to be in that moving thing – even if it was to take us to see my dad.

Mother usually woke up early in the mornings and after saying prayers out loud, she would light the fire and prepare our meal. After we ate, she and I made our way down the road to our plot of land. I would always have a book with me and loved to share this time with my mother. The fields seemed vast to my inexperienced eyes and I often wanted to help till the land and bring in the harvest.

Some days, our job would be to clear and clean the rows that the next crop would be planted in. Upon our arrival, Mother would place our belongings under the tall shade tree and make her way to a pile of digging hoes. I would follow her, eager to help as best I could. I would, however, also bring a book with me to read during our midday break. The stories would be fresh in my mind and I would be eager to return to them as soon as I was through helping my mother tend the fields. Someday, this would be my job so I needed to learn it well.

But one day I reached out for a hoe and my mother grabbed my wrist. Mother hadn't let me help yet, and I thought that this was the day. I started, wondering what I'd done wrong and what kind of punishment it might warrant. I was old enough and strong enough, surely she could see this. When I tentatively looked into her eyes, it was not anger I saw, but understanding and a wisdom I have come to associate with motherhood and long life.

A question was ready to spill from my lips but it seemed she already knew that I didn't understand and began to speak before I stuttered my question.

"No, Njoki, these are not for you," Mother said.

Not for me? Are there other small hoes I could use? I wondered.

"What do you mean, Mama? I want to help you," I asked.

Her smile reassured me that I hadn't made a mistake, at least not one that I shouldn't have. I appreciated these rare moments where my mother was all mine and I didn't have to share her with anyone else. As wife and mother, my mother was often busy with many tasks. At that particular moment, she looked at me like I was her only baby and I couldn't help but smile back at her, feeling much younger than I did a moment ago.

"I know you do. But you are not meant to help in the fields," Mother said.

"Why not, Mama? I am strong enough. I can help you!"

I could see the appreciation in her eyes, but it was not clear what she wanted me to do. Mother released my hand and knelt down beside me. Her movements were graceful as she lowered herself to the ground. She was every bit the chief's daughter. Despite my father being a government officer, the provider, my mother was the one that held the power in our homestead.

Her father, my grandfather, was a chief of our village; my mother's brother also became a chief. My grandmother was the youngest wife and held much power and influence in our small community. I can still remember the many evenings I spent at my grandmother's house where she shared many stories about our traditions. Now and then, she would turn to me with a worried look, concerned that I might never truly appreciate where my family has come from. However, she would still go on and say at the end of each story, "My granddaughter, never, ever forget your roots or where you came from."

My mother was as close to me as she ever had been. I could see the warmth in her eyes as she took my palm and ran her fingers over the lines and then down my fingers. When she looked back up at me, she smiled and said, "My Njoki, touch my hands."

She held out her hands, palms up in offering and I took the opportunity to really examine each ridge and plane. Her hands were rough from working the fields and tending our home. There were calluses on her fingers, some blisters on her palms in various stages of healing and faint burns from working the fires over the years. They were a woman's hands, I decided; a woman who worked hard for her family and her village. I have to pause again to calm myself down – I still remember that moment. I can still see my mother – I wrap my hands together, they are soft and tears flow as I remember my mother's hands. And in particular when she said, "What do you feel?"

"Your hands are rough from work, Mama. They are very rough, Mama...you should oil your hands."

"Yes, yes. They are rough from work; hard work and long days. This is my path, my destiny."

I nodded, understanding as much as I could. My mother's hands were evidence of the life she had chosen and the path that was offered to her. They represented everything she was: strong and skilled, rough but capable.

"Now, Njoki, touch your hands. What do you feel?"

I already knew the answer to this, but I did as I was told, anyway. My hands were smooth, long-fingered and nimble. There was none of the strength my mother's hands had and I knew they were certainly less skilled. I spent most of my time reading books, playing with my dear friend Patricia and causing all the mischief children were meant to cause.

"Mama, my hands are smooth. I've done no work like you."

"You are right. My hands are not meant to be your hands, little Njoki. My path has taken me to the fields and the fire. Yours will take you to books and school. That is what I want for you. I do this now so you won't have to cultivate under the hot sun or go in search of firewood. You are meant for more than this." Mother ran her fingers on a page of my book and said to me, "Do you see these little figures all over the page? Master them . . . they are your hoes. If you know them well, they will provide for you. They will not let you down. They do not have seasons like we have here . . . rain season, dry season . . . mmm but you need to prepare and plan just like the way I do for my shamba – my family plot – and be committed and focused."

Though Mother spoke the words softly, the reverence in her voice made the meaning sit heavy in my belly. I had told Patricia so many times that I wanted to be a professor when I grew up. I really didn't know what that meant, but I was certain I wanted it. Now, hearing my mother wanted these things for me was like hearing a prophecy told. My mother wanted this for me. I had never seen something she had ordered fail to happen, so it must be my path.

A smile broke across my face in understanding. I told myself, I must study. I must read and I must never stop learning. This was my path.

Mother said, "Now, go sit under that shade tree and read. When it is time to eat, I will join you and you will read to me from your book. Remember where we left off before. I want to know what happens next."

Mother was tall and beautiful. I knew that she took pride in her family and our accomplishments. Mother had long ago confessed to me that she didn't like conflict – or gossip. She loved peace and she would do everything to maintain peace in her family.

I'd heard some of the girls in my village say that my mother was proud and stayed away because she didn't want to be part of the village community. I knew Mother more than those girls. She was my mother and for me, that was the most important thing. Mother had all the qualities that one would wish to see in her mother. As I write about Mother, I am truly emotional. I wish she was here today, now, as I have so many questions to ask her about mother-hood. My eyes are full of tears – Mum, why did you have to die so early?

Where my father had taken on some aspects of the Western lifestyle, my mother was traditional and patient. They called him a Mzungu, a white man, because of how he carried himself and the clothes he wore. Father was always dressed in a suit; and his focus was on putting all his hard-earned salary into educating his children. Many people in the village thought of him as a poor man because he did not own a shop like many government officers in the village did; instead, he owned a bicycle.

From that day on, what was once a funny habit became a tradition filled with meaning. My mother tended the land while I studied under the tree from the books my brothers and sisters brought home for me. When midday came, Mother would take her rest and her meal with me under the tree. I took special care each day to mark the place in the book that we had stopped the day before.

I felt such joy in those moments, being allowed to see my mother relaxed and happy as I read each story to her. I loved how she grew to love each character and would rant and rave when they did things she didn't want them to do. I had accepted my role – to become my mother's eyes with which she would read and know about the world outside the village, faraway lands . . . the Americas. I wish Mother was here today, because I would share my stories with her, not about America, but Canada. My home and the home of her grandchildren and great-grandchildren.

On our way home, we talked about the stories and she told me her opinions, what should happen next and how she would have told the story differently. These times were the most animated and it was amazing to listen to her analysis of the events from a novel she was "reading" through my eyes. I almost regretted returning home and watching that seriousness come over her again. I knew that she would not be so open until the next time we read.

I craved the times when I would get to see my mother as a carefree woman, wrapped up in a story. I hoped I would be as strong as her someday, as skilled and as disciplined. And, I hoped I would get to learn far more than she had but not to know more than her. I hoped to learn so I could continue to teach. Under that tree, in the coffee fields, I had been given a gift.

Instead of being little Njoki, I had become Professor Njoki, teaching my mother from my books, and I wanted this feeling again, I wanted this feeling forever. I pause and think of her:

> Woman of fields, oh my mother, I am thinking of you.
> Mother, woman who never complained, I miss you.
> Mum, the shoulders of whom I stand on today, forgive
>   me;
> Mother, who died alone, forgive me for not being at
>   your bedside as you took your last breath.
> Forgive me for my tears; they are tears of love and
>   appreciation.
> Mother, in spirit we are together.
> Mother, in spirit I read for you.
> I read for you from what I have written.
> I read for you what you taught me.
> I read for you though it is painful to remember these
>   moments.
> Mother, you are love and I thank you for your teachings.
> Mother, you will always, always be in my heart.

Writing: The Rituals of Academia

A major responsibility of university professors is to conduct and publish original research or other academic papers. It is our duty as experts in the field to contribute to the body of work that continues to advance and improve our field of study. During my time at the university, I've enjoyed the privilege of publishing with a number of honoured and respected colleagues.

But writing has also become a pleasure of mine and was modelled for me very early in life. My father used to write all the time, every day in fact, and I've enjoyed those times in my life when I've had the time and focus to emulate that habit. I've always wondered what he wrote in that journal of his.

Academic articles are a way for researchers to express their thoughts and theories, sometimes through the scientific process and other times by challenging or evaluating works that are already in existence. I've learned over the years that some great discussions have erupted from the evaluation of older works, whose theories have become outdated.

But research and article writing can also be an exhausting process involving posturing and politics as often as examining long-standing academic theories. Ideally, the controversy would serve to improve a body of work and enhance the accuracy of any research. Unfortunately, it is often more about someone not wanting to be wrong rather than wanting to find the truth.

In society, it is even more difficult for people to let go of a faulty idea. It may take years or even decades to fully believe that it is time to let our assumptions and conclusions go in the face of new evidence. I love the thrill of academic debate because, when done correctly, you can change the minds of a room full of people through a carefully constructed argument or counter-argument and the diplomatic presentation of a new way of thinking.

I've written articles on everything from spirituality to the cultural adaptation of people who are new to an environment, to feminisms, to traditional healing. Each time I sit down to begin an article, I appreciate what a privilege it is to have a degree and the support of my university to get my thoughts out into the academic world. In a way, it's like writing in my journal or thinking through a course that I would like to teach. I take time to think through the material, and reflect on what I want to write or offer in the course.

Most of the time, the intent of the work is to develop and understand the philosophical basis of different topics and their implication for education. Given the heterogeneity of ideas that run through my brain, I see my writing or my courses as a way to create a space for dialogue with readers or students. Not all articles have to be an accumulation of facts and figures. Some theoretical articles are more exploratory and allow the authors to ask questions without necessarily providing the answers to those questions. You write to the reader and encourage them to consider that what they believe to be true may not be quite accurate. However, sometimes, I just journal for myself – just like Dad did for many years.

Journaling has become a favourite assignment of mine for my students, as well. I'll often have them examine some controversial or thought-provoking questions or statements, take the day to consider and then have them write down whatever comes up. I always explain to them that they should view this exercise as having a conversation with themselves or with their professor and that they should not worry about references or quoting other people's work. I encourage them to take time at the end of each class to critically engage in a reflective exercise with the day's readings, class discussion, their own thoughts and to write it all down in their journals.

These entries may be in the form of issues raised by the various authors in our reading and how these authors positioned their ideas in relation to the topics being discussed. They may also be in the form of questions – questions that were not fully explored in class or questions that were not raised in class or questions that may be exploratory in nature and may not have any one answer.

It would be tempting to have the students turn these entries in after each class. However, making this activity into a cumbersome or uncomfortable assignment often limits the range of responses the student might have. When journaling feels like something they *have* to do, I often get pages and pages of what they think I want to hear. Only some of the students, most likely already familiar with the concept, will delve deep and explore the various levels of my questions.

The alternative is to have only two journal submissions. This prevents them from becoming repetitive and superficial as they run out of ideas when they get tired and distracted. But, some students will journal each time they are prompted, and sometimes more than I ask them to, learning to explore their own mind through free writing.

I've found it quite a fascinating exercise to write in a journal when I'm frustrated, angry or sad and come back to it later and reread my entry. I've learned so much about how I think when I'm upset, motivated and moved by something or when I sit in a coffee house and write down what tends to bother me with relative consistency and what kind of memories those emotions tend to provoke.

My students will do the same for their entries and I can often tell when something has "hit home" or triggered a belief or value that is especially dear to them. The content of the journal is not necessarily what I am interested in. The purpose of my lectures is not to teach the students to think the way I think or believe what I believe. I want them to develop a certain level of comfort and familiarity with their own minds and how they work through ideas, problems or challenging moments.

We tend to repeat the behaviours we are most familiar with and not the ones that we necessarily wish we'd repeat. I want these students to practise problem solving, self-evaluation and non-judgmental exploration of alternative beliefs, values and cultures. In order for me to know that's happening I either need to hear them do it in class or see them do it in assignments.

In primary school, I would often write home, telling my family what was happening and informing them of struggles and triumphs. I remember writing down my frustrations, my ambitions and my sadness being so far from home, and then, since I could not erase what I'd already written, explore and mediate my frustrations right there in the letter.

I didn't want my family to see me as unhappy, so whenever I would write about a concern or difficulty, I would do my best to solve it as well. I remember feeling a measure of relief after completing each letter, not just because I'd had the opportunity to express myself, but because I'd had the opportunity to problem solve, as well.

Of course, there's always the fear of criticism or rejection. You can never tell when an idea will be well received or vehemently challenged. There are times when I wish I could keep all my writings to myself, protecting myself from that hurt of rejection. Sometimes the fear of being judged by others is so strong that my fingers simply stop on the keyboard, refusing to type another letter until I've resolved whatever issue has come up.

Eventually I find my courage again, often through my peers and co-authors. Their encouragement and support make me braver and more determined than I might ever be on my own. Some part of me rebels against the idea of being dependent on someone else for strength, but I long ago learned that sometimes, you simply cannot walk a path by yourself. Sometimes you need someone to hold the torch while you carry the load.

I wonder what it would feel like for someone to read my journal entries and critique them the way they would my academic papers.

Would I still be so strong?

Some thoughts are meant to stay private and others are simply not safe in the hands of others. We all struggle and fight and think things we should not think or feel things we wish we didn't feel. The nuns would have called such things a sin, but I know now that the thoughts themselves are impossible to stop. Our power is in what we choose to do with those thoughts.

Do we feed them? Encourage them to multiply?

Or, do we acknowledge their existence but give them no energy by which to take root and grow?

Journaling can be a way of acknowledging thoughts and feelings without feeding them: like depositing something in a safe, you must first take inventory before you lock it all away. Otherwise, you never quite know what to expect when you open the safe another day.

Father's Journal

My father was old when my brother and I were born.

I liked listening to his stories of adventure. He told us that he remembered when the white men first came to Kenya; he was a boy then. Baba was probably ninety years old when he told us this story. Some of the children I used to play with in the village used to call my dad an old man; they would tease me and refer to him as my grandfather, but I didn't really see the difference between my father and theirs. Why was his age so important?

I sometimes used to wonder if he felt part of our village or more like a visitor, as he was away when we were children. Yet I knew our home was important to him. I knew he enjoyed spending time with us, all gathered around the fire in the courtyard, telling stories and making us laugh with his crafty tales.

Father was an orphan, and though he didn't speak much about it, I often wondered whether he was curious about the people who created him. He was found abandoned, with no record or clues as to where he came from. From the stories that have been passed down, Baba was a few weeks old when his adoptive family found him. A couple who could bear no children found him and adopted him. Later when white men came to our village looking for house help, my dad's adoptive parents gave him away. It was in his new home that my father learned how to read and write, and when my father's boss got a transfer to Mombasa, eight hundred kilometres from Embu, to lay telephone cables, Dad went with him.

In 1919, after the First World War, my dad's boss got transferred to Britain, and because my father had become part of his family, he paid for my father's sea passage to Britain. However, on the day the ship was going to sail, Dad was inside the ship with some friends who had come to say goodbye to him. They convinced him to abandon his adventure, because "white people were different" and they had been known to take people to slavery. Maybe, they told Dad, he was going to be a slave.

Dad got scared, although he did not show it. After his friends left and the ship was slowly wading its way from the port, Dad jumped, swam ashore and started his eight hundred kilometre trek back to Embu. As soon as he got back to Embu, he was employed to train soldiers for the colonial government. This was because of his education, but also because he had travelled to different countries during the First World War to fight for the colonial government. It was then that he met his first wife, Maatha, and got married in 1921.

Nine years later, he decided to change his career and enrolled in a three-year veterinary college program. On his return, he got a job as a veterinary officer, in charge of Embu District. However, people did not trust him and many of them did not allow him to treat their animals. This was because he was a colonial government employee. People from the village thought he was on the side of the colonial government. It was because of that mistrust that Dad decided to change his strategy and instead trained to be an agricultural officer, becoming a household name, the person who could be consulted for anything to do with farming methods, whether it was cattle keeping, beehive keeping, artificial insemination for animals or plant grafting. He believed in our freedom and he did not want people to call him or even think he was a traitor. If anyone wanted exotic seeds, they knew where to get them – from my dad.

He became the veterinary doctor – the doctor whom they had rejected, but who was actually employed as a veterinary officer by the Ministry of Livestock and Animal Husbandry. Today, some of the plants we have in Embu were introduced by my dad; however, we have no idea where he got them.

Because he often travelled, I spent far less time with my father than my mother, leaving him quite mysterious to me. My favourite times were when we all gathered in the courtyard in front of the main house, lit a fire and sat around it listening to my father tell us the stories he'd collected from around the country.

From him, we learnt of other villages and cities, people he'd met and adventures he'd had. My father was a wonderful storyteller and had our rapt attention until the fire burnt low and we were all sent inside for the evening. Though he'd only be home for a few weeks at a time, my father's presence was with us in his absence. His word was law: a law enforced by my mother. Between my father's two wives and all their children, our household was quite full and I know that my father relied on my mother to keep the peace and make sure everything got done as he expected it to be.

While my mother wore the simple dresses and head wraps that were common among the women in my village, my father wore a suit every day. He often spoke out against the more traditional ways of living, challenging the chief and the elders in the village.

Of all my father's habits, the one I found most interesting was his morning ritual. Each morning, my father rose from his bed, washed from the bowl of water my mother set out for him and dressed for the day in one of his suits. My mother got up earlier than him to prepare his water and his meal so that when my father woke up he could move through his morning routine without delay.

After washing and dressing, he would head to the kitchen table where my mother set out his meal. Dad took his time to contemplate on issues – not sure what – but he remained silent as he ate his meal and went through his diary. All of this was entertaining enough for a little girl like me but what truly piqued my curiosity was the journal he wrote in after his breakfast.

Once my mother took the dishes to the kitchen, my father would fetch his journal and pen and begin to write. Whenever I asked him what he wrote, he would only smile and shake his head. Clearly what was in there was not meant for me but his adamant denial only served to bolster my wonder even more.

What could he possibly be writing in there?

Did he ever write about me?

Is it good?

Is it bad?

What if it was all bad stuff?

Each question led to another question and I often found myself spending hours talking to Patricia and Elena about the magic that must be in my father's journal. We all used to take turns telling each other stories about what he wrote. Sometimes we would speculate it was about secret missions for the government, other times we thought he wrote all the knowledge he had of the Veterinary Department and how to take care of animals. Sometimes, we thought it was about his visits with the spirits. Sometimes it was about all the wonderful fruits he brought home from his travels and other times it was about whether or not war was coming to Kenya.

We seemed to alternate between the certainty that my father had a book full of fabulous secrets and the notion that his journal was full of drawings that he made while convincing us that he was writing everything down. I knew it must be important. My father would never waste a moment of his time and I couldn't imagine that he would take the time to write something down if it didn't matter.

But, why didn't he want any of us to know what was in there?

Did it matter if we knew?

He wouldn't write anything bad about us in there, would he?

Eventually, I had to move on to another fantasy but as always, each morning when he sat down and wrote in his journal, I'd start wondering all over again. Perhaps someday I'd be allowed to read his journal. I knew he kept every book he filled somewhere in his bedroom. I believed there would come a day when he had no more use for that collection of journals and we would finally get to find out what my father had been thinking about all these years.

Until then, we made up stories.

There was one week when Patricia and I imagined that my father was writing about his time spent exploring the moon and all the fruits that grew there. We were sure that that was where many of the pale fruits came from. Elena seemed doubtful, but she had yet to come up with a better idea so our idea stayed for now.

Another week, we decided that my father was writing letters to my mother that she read once he left the house. After hours of pretending to be my mother, reading love letters from my father, I realized that we had come up with a possibility that might actually be true. Suddenly, I was filled with joy and happiness at the idea that my father spent each morning writing letters to my mother. He was gone so often, I often wondered whether or not she missed him as much as we children did.

My mother was so calm and serious most of the time, I could never tell what she really felt unless she was upset with me or we were in the field reading. Those times were so precious to me that I didn't dare waste a second of it on silly questions about my father's writings.

What if she did know what he wrote about?

What if she read the journals when he'd gone, even when she was not supposed to?

What would my father have done if he ever found out?

I realized the flaw in my reasoning when it occurred to me that my mother didn't know how to read very well, and what little she could read usually seemed to annoy her. I doubted she could spend that much time reading my father's journal and not improve in her reading elsewhere.

Again, I was left with the mystery of the journal and I couldn't seem to tear my mind away. While at the river with my friends Patricia and Muikaria, we began to write in our own journals, making squiggles and shapes in the soft sand by the river. I drew a box around mine making it look like a piece of paper and dated each entry. When the river rose or someone walked by, these "diaries" would be washed away and we would have to start all over the next day.

Someday, when I learnt how to write, I told myself, I would be able to keep my journal entries in a book like my father did. When I do, I told myself, I would invite my children to read them as I did not want to keep any secrets. Everything I would write down would be for other people to read, I told myself.

I wanted everyone to know what I thought. Patricia, Elena and I decided that we would write all kinds of books when we grew up, with pictures and wonderful stories just like the ones my father used to tell us around the fire at night.

Everyone would love our stories and want to share them with their families, too. I couldn't wait to have my first journal, to write down all the things I thought of, all the things I wanted to say out loud and never got the chance to because I was little and no one listened to little children for very long. I'd be a storyteller and a writer, just like my father.

I couldn't wait!

Now I have lots of diaries: I have written them since I was in grade nine. Reading those diaries today, I laugh. I am amused by the things that occupied my life then and now. I have also written academic books and articles. I am, however, not so sure they are as fun to read.

Graduation

If standing in front of a room full of students as a professor was one of the proudest moments of my life, then standing in front of an auditorium full of graduates as a tenured professor surely has to be even better. The large room is filled with happy parents, excited students, colourful banners and signs and the occasional, pre-ceremony air horn.

Each time I walk down the aisles in a procession for a graduating class, my eyes well with tears and I become emotional. The procession makes its way to the dais in our Convocation Hall and we all turn to watch as students walk to the chancellor or the president of the university who will shake their hand and congratulate them on their achievement. The dais, which faces the audience where the students, their parents and friends sit, is a space preserved for faculty and senior administers of the university. The professors wear the robes and hoods of the university from which they graduated. I wear the University of Toronto robe and hood, which is black and decorated with wide stripes of red and white piping.

I simply love seeing the professors, from many different universities, come together in this space, on this stage to acknowledge the next generation of graduates. But my proudest moments are those when one of the students graduating has worked with me for the past two, four, five or sometimes even six years; I find it quite incredible.

I feel like a mother, sending my children off into the world to find their own way. The pride I have for each one of them brings tears to my eyes, and I wave at them or give them hugs as they cross the stage, all in the hope that they know how much I feel for them. These ceremonies are notoriously long and I wonder where I get the energy to cry this much every year, as my joyful heart makes the hours seem like minutes.

When the names are being called, I wait with bated breath until they call a name that I recognize. Even more exciting are the moments when the student crossing the stage has become familiar to me over hours of tutoring, mentoring or campus activities. Bits of term papers, questions from lectures and hallway conversations flit through my mind as I see each familiar face like a highlight reel of our sweetest moments, playing out behind my welling eyes.

Do they notice my joy?

As a daughter of a very large family, I know that time spent in each other's thoughts is just as important as time spent in the same room.

Honestly, I have children of my own to worry about but as I see these young people, walking down the hallways laughing and playing as children do, I see myself in them and find myself wanting for them what my mother wanted for me. It makes sense that a mother thinks of her children all the time ... and within the African cosmology, we think of our community children as our children. We become other mothers.

It's an honoured position if a demanding one, to be the person a child thinks of when they're scared and need help. It's a mark of true trust and love. I hope my children think of me when they struggle to understand the challenges a man or woman faces in this world. I hope they think of me when someone asks them a question they don't know the answer to.

I also endeavour to teach my students how to care about more than what they've experienced first-hand, and perhaps even how to be honest and honourable in the face of the unknown.

After receiving emails, having students arrive at office hours and being surrounded by questions after the lecture, I've learned to accept that my topics are provocative and not always easily received.

This next student is one such individual. His name is Leo. He struggled in the beginning. Now look at him! He walks across the stage with such enthusiasm, waving to his friends and family, smiling brightly.

Leo has grown so much these past six years. I wonder if he is even aware of how different he is from the young man that first walked into my graduate seminar on Cultural Knowledges and Representation, tucking himself in the furthest corner and hoping no one would notice him. He's blossomed into a confident, knowledgeable young man, ready to face the next stage of life as recipient of a Ph.D. degree from our university.

I've heard many colleagues voice their observations to students they mentor, and each time their words are met with polite gratitude. I suppose it is difficult to see yourself the way others might see you.

Those are the times when we practise being who we want to be. And then, when a challenge comes along, we fall back on those habits and beliefs we've most practised, not necessarily the ones we most value. I try to reflect those moments back to my students as often as possible. It is their best chance to stay on the right path, rather than waiting until crisis befalls them and they are unable to cope.

Leo is about ready to walk offstage and I wave to him, knowing some part of him will know how proud I am, whether he sees me or not.

Suddenly he turns, looks right at me and reveals a face-splitting grin and waves at me.

"Thank you," he whispers.

"You are welcome."

The Long Walk to School

The first day of going to my new school has stayed with
me.

I was going to a real school, away from home. This
was surely the best thing that's ever happened to me. After
years of reading to Mother in the fields, I was finally being
allowed to study away from home and I promised Mother
to read every book they told me to. I was going to Sacred
Heart Girls School. I was not going back to my old school
– the Ena Primary School. I had heard from some of the
other children that the nuns who would teach us were Ital-
ians, but I was not really sure why that mattered. The walk
to the new school took Mother and I the whole day and I
can still recall how anxious I was to get going.

Mother had helped me pack my suitcase the previous night and I had stared at it all night while trying desperately to sleep. I had a new name, a new school and a new place to live during the school year. Everything I needed had been tucked away in that little suitcase and I could hardly believe that so little would last so long. Determination flooded my body. I remember promising myself to learn everything they taught us and then I would bring it home in the summer and teach Mother, as well. I was sure she would be very proud.

I knew other girls from the village were also going to school that day, as well. Until that time, we had all been attending Ena Primary School. I loved my time there, especially the last year when I got to play a princess in a school play. I can still remember the little blue dress that I wore, which my sister Mary had made for me. I was excited because I was going to see Wambere, our neighbour's daughter. Her mother was our primary school teacher and her father was an education officer. Wambere had changed her name like I did. I hoped I'd remember to call her Ella instead of Wambere.

When we were finally ready to go, I was overcome with an excitement that made the early morning hour seem completely unimportant. When we set out, the sun had just risen, bringing with it the first licks of warmth to the new day. Walking on the main road at that hour was a peaceful walk and I took my time memorizing the details that I saw. I knew, after we crossed the Ena Bridge, Mother would take a shortcut through bushes. I had been on that path many times going to the Indian market with my mother, but that day was different. I was not going to the Indian stores to witness my mother searching for bargains; on that day, I was going to a new school.

As always, the path was narrow and dusty and the January heat began to bear down on us. I wished it was in March after the rains or in June when the weather was cool. We talked about the year to come, what I hoped to learn and I promised my mother again and again to bring back all the knowledge I gathered over the year and share it with her. She smiled at me each time I said it and I knew she was looking forward to that time already.

Mother had my suitcase perched on her head and I did not envy the weight of it though the shade might be nice. Patricia and I had practised balancing imaginary water bowls on our heads many times but balancing a suitcase was something I had neglected to practise in our playtime. We stopped only a couple of times for water as my stomach was far too nervous to tolerate more than the small meal we ate before leaving home.

The terrain was all familiar to me. I had walked on this same path a month ago to take back my acceptance forms to the school. My younger brother came with me and we played the whole way; we had a good time. However, today was different. I had dreamt of this walk many times since then, imagining my journey to the tall, imposing building, the likes of which I had never seen before. The stones seemed cold, all dark grey and impossibly heavy. I was certain this place could withstand any storm, no matter the rain or wind.

By the end of the day, that school would be my home along with all the girls I saw signing up that day. I imagined that we would all be as close as sisters, playing and laughing and learning together. Perhaps there would be time for imaginary games, like the ones I played with Patricia. We had been practising holding babies with a blanket bundle, gathering water from the river and dancing as often as we could.

I doubted there would be a river full of crocodiles like the Ena River once we got to school, but I was certain there would be an adventure to be had. With all those children in one place, I thought, there must be all kinds of games to play and people to play them with.

My excitement built as we caught our first glimpse of my new school off in the distance. The heat rose from the ground making the sturdy walls appear to dance and sway to an ancient rhythm. I imagined myself dancing with it, laughing in delight as I learnt the steps from a place that must be so much older and wiser than I.

I wondered whether I could call this place home. Could it be home? Would it ever be home? I would not mind living here all my life.

I told myself, I would ask when we arrived.

The closer we got, the more detail became visible. My smile began to drop as the walls of the school stopped dancing and I was able to see all the activity in front of its endless steps. Cars of every shape and colour were moving about the base of the staircase. Some were like the old ones I had seen in the village or at the market and others seemed more special somehow.

I wondered if they were more expensive or newer.

My curiosity quickly shifted from the cars to their occupants and my breath caught in my chest as I recognized the dress of one of the little girls climbing out of one of those polished black cars.

It is the neighbour's daughter Wanjiku. I turned to my mother, about to make a comment when I saw the look on her face.

My mother was seeing none of what I saw. That was clear.

The look of pride in her eyes made my chest tight and tears prick at the corner of my eyes. My shock turned quickly to anger and then settled with a thud in embarrassment. Our neighbours could have offered to give us a ride to school, but they did not. And here I was, walking barefoot in the dirt, next to my mother who was carrying my suitcase on her head like a common village woman.

How could I have been so foolish?

I should have asked for a ride with one of the other girls. Surely one of my friends would have allowed me to travel with them. I cannot believe I did not think of this sooner. This was going to be the one thing everyone remembered about me for the rest of the school year. I could hear them all now:

Oh you? You, little Njoki? Or is it Catherine? You are the one who came to school with your mother carrying your suitcase on her head. Too poor to drive? Of course, you are that old man's daughter!

Their laughter echoed in my ears like a prophecy of what was to come. I didn't even bother to argue that they couldn't possibly know all of that about me yet but still, I was overcome with pain. The damage was already done and there was nothing else I could do but send my mother on her way as quickly as possible. As we approached the school, I tugged quickly and quietly at my mother's arm, desperately begging without the words that might draw the attention of the other girls for her to put my suitcase down and just *go*.

It was not working. She gently set my suitcase down and took her time observing the crowd and the large building. I didn't know if she had ever seen such a thing before and I was certainly not going to ask now. She was embarrassing me and needed to go!

I hated this feeling. I should not have been angry at my mother for being proud of me, but it seemed simply too much to ask when my own emotions ran so high. Doing my best to not make eye contact with any of the other girls, I shook hands with my mother, grabbed my suitcase and rushed off to join my year mates. I dragged my suitcase behind me and I dared not look back to my mother or the other parents who were there to see their children off.

I wondered if I'd regret, someday, not taking the time to hear what she said to me before she turned to make the walk home.

As I write this story, I have to stop – it is really emotional for me – the pain of loss and lack of appreciation overwhelms me. These moments have haunted me for many years.

Why do we as human beings turn our backs on what is ours? Why do we reject the very centre of our being? Looking back, my mother was my first teacher, the only person who loved me unconditionally. She was so proud of me; proud of me even when I failed her. I returned in August 2018 and visited Sacred Heart Girls School. The image of my mother was overwhelming. I stood still, and asked her to forgive me. To take me back as I am, her daughter who is so proud of her mother, the mother around whom my whole world revolves.

Mother, take my hand and hold it tight!
Let's make another entrance to my new school.
Look at me again, Mother.
What do you see?
Do you see my admiration for you?
Do you see that I want to show off my mother?
Do you hear me calling my friends to come, yes
Come and meet my mother?
The woman without whom my world would be
    nothing?
Mother, that day, your selfish daughter
Did not want anything about you, of you.
But today, I want everything about you:
Your grace, warmth, gentleness, patience!

But I couldn't be bothered at that time. There was so much to do and so much to see. That day was not about her, it was about me and my school year.

We were all gathered together by the nuns and directed to small groups of the older girls. I pulled my suitcase closer and prepared to make my way inside. I hoped I would get to stop in my room before going to dinner. I wanted to put my suitcase away and wash.

Later, I wondered if Mother made it home before dark.

Mama, the woman of the mountains
Please forgive me
Mama, I was a child then, and am still your child now
I love you, Mama, and will always do
Woman of grace
My mother, I am thinking of you
I see you, Mama, just like it was yesterday
I am thinking of you
Mama, I long for you
Mama, I long for your touch
Mama, I long for your warm, rough hands
Mama, please visit me
Visit me in my dreams
I want to hear your voice once again
Mama, this time, I will listen
This time, I will hang on to everything you say
Mama, you will always be my Mama, the woman of the
    fields
Mama, let me share with you my first night away from
    you

My First Bed:
A Shifting Bed

The most exciting gift I received at the Sacred Heart Girls School was the pleasure of my very own bed. After a long day's walk, enduring the embarrassment of my mother carrying my suitcase on her head, and the overwhelming novelty of the Catholic nuns and their towering school, I was surely ready to collapse.

I had spent my entire life sharing a bed with at least two other people. My father had a bed of his own but my mother, my younger brother Njeru and I shared a bed and I would be hard pressed to miss it given the sheer wonder of this new place. Though the homemade mattress and familiar hanging in our bedroom would be welcome now to soothe my lingering anxiety, I felt new life rushing into me as I was directed to my very own little bed.

How wonderful!

There was no sense in embarrassing myself any further today so I kept my shock and excitement to myself. There were fifty girls in each dormitory, twenty-five up against one wall and twenty-five against the other and none of them would have to bear witness to any more of my mistakes today. No one had made any comments yet, but I remembered the taunting words in my own mind and was just waiting to hear them stated out loud.

Keeping my head down, I dragged my suitcase behind me and followed the other girls into the dormitory. The older girls were unpacking their cases but making no noise. I quickly learnt why when a nun explained to us in our own language that there was to be no talking.

How strange!

Seeing the wisdom of not breaking rules on the very first day, or at all for that matter, I kept my mouth shut and gathered as much information as I could with my eyes. The feet of each of the beds, which were placed side by side, created a walkway down the middle of the room. At the end of that walkway was where the who's who of the children slept: the commissioners' daughters and other children of important people. Their beds were stacked (I later found out these were called double-decker beds) one on top of the other with plush-looking mattresses, pillows, blankets and a little place for their belongings.

I suppose the difference in sleeping spaces should have bothered me but I couldn't seem to care as one of the nuns nudged me to my bed. She said something in a language I didn't understand – English, one of the other girls said –

and nodded her head in the direction of the empty beds. Realizing that this one was going to be mine for the rest of the year, I quickly placed my suitcase beside the bed and began to unpack all that I had brought with me. I had less than ten items in the small suitcase.

As instructed I'd brought two blankets and two sheets and we all rushed to make our beds. The process was unfamiliar to me, and I peeped out of the corner of my eyes to watch how the older girls made quick work of their task. Sheets were folded and draped across the top of the bed and then the blankets go on top of that. But these two wooden planks bothered me a little bit – not much – they were hard and narrow – but what did it matter? It was my bed, my first bed.

Not too difficult, I thought and set to work, arranging my own little place to rest.

I folded the sheets in half as best I could but they were longer than I was tall and I struggled with them for a moment before figuring out how to manoeuvre the long material. The blankets offered similar resistance and when I finished, I looked around to see if anyone else had the difficulty I did. Other girls were still battling with too-long sheets and I was relieved that my experience was not an isolated one.

As the sun set, the light from the little windows began to yellow and fade. Through a flurry of orders from one stern-faced, elderly nun and translation from another, we were sent to bed. Too scared and excited to say anything, I settled under my blankets and desperately tried to ignore the rumbling in my belly. Apparently, we were all expected to have eaten before making our way to school. And despite my pitiful morning nibbles, it was now clear to me that I would be sleeping on an empty tummy tonight.

I turned on my side, away from the window and gazed over the rows of little girls in front of me. We all looked the same in the meagre light except for our blankets; each one a colourful marker of where we came from and who loved us enough to ensure we got an education in this place for girls only. Of course, my mother bought my blankets and the sudden thought of her sent a mix of loneliness and anger running through my heart. I wriggled around on my bed, as if to fend off the emotion she brought, before settling back into sleep.

My breathing deepened and my thoughts slowed down. The novelty of the day receded and, for a moment, my eyelids drooped. The dorm was now pitch black as the moon had yet to rise and my tired eyes made shapes out of imaginary shadows to entertain me. Just as the exhaustion of the long day began to take over, my eyelids becoming heavy and my limbs tingling pleasantly with the whispers of sleep, something shifted.

Oh my God! What was that?

Perhaps the guilt of my mother's silent departure would not let me rest. I rolled over to my other side, now facing the window and settled into my blankets, once more burrowing in and tugging the blankets up to my ears. The swirl of colour behind my eyelids began to darken and sleep was, once again, about to take over.

Another odd shift.

What in the world was going on?

Was the school moving?

I had never felt such a thing before, especially when I was the only one in bed. I half expected to look next to me and see my mother on one side and brother Njeru fidgeting in his sleep, but I knew that was not the case. I was at school. They were both at home with my other brothers and sisters. This was my bed and no one else's. As I pressed myself up with a hand, rising up on my side, there was another mighty shift, the screech of wood sliding on wood, and suddenly my bed parted beneath me and I fell to the floor in a heap.

Shock stopped me from truly understanding what had just happened, but it didn't last long. It wasn't a long fall, just an unexpected one and there was only a little pain in my hip where it hit the concrete floor. As I looked around me, first seeing the state of my sleeping space and then the faces of my year-mates looking at me with trepidation in the moonlight, I understood what had occurred.

It was really quite ridiculous and I began to giggle.

How fun!

It would seem that the bed was not a bed at all, at least not one that I had seen before. There were two wooden pedestals at the head and the foot of the bed. On top of these pedestals were two wooden planks set side by side, creating a pallet for us to sleep on. Apparently, with all my shifting and huffing, the planks had separated below me, allowing me to fall right between them, blankets, sheets and all.

I sat in a little sinkhole, a little bundle of Njoki and bedsheets, simply elated by my discovery.

As my giggles turned to full belly laughs, the other girls began to join me, relieved to see that I was unharmed and that no one would have to fetch a nun for help. Some even wiggled around in their beds until their planks separated and they disappeared in a whoosh of sheets and blankets.

Over and over again, we all jumped back up, gathered our blankets and remade our beds, which had now turned into a most unexpectedly delightful game. The woes of the day disappeared under the light-filled wash of children's laughter and I was once again so happy to be at school, surrounded by other girls and the heady anticipation of what was to come.

Our exhaustion was only delayed for so long before laughter once again reduced to giggles, then smiles and finally happy yawns. We made our beds for the final time and allowed sleep to take us. I would admit, however, that the sound of another little girl accidentally falling between the planks of her bed later that night was just as funny the twentieth time as it was the first.

What was less fun was waking up the next morning with bruised shoulders, scraped knees, too little sleep and too many things to pay attention to. In my previous delight, I hadn't realized that such a hard bed of two planks would take a toll on me, nor did I realize just how rough a concrete floor could be on the tender skin of palms and kneecaps.

It was a lesson I was sure I'd need more than once because, even as I hissed at the sting when I touched the scrapes or pressed at the bruises, a smile crept over my lips and I couldn't wait for bedtime once again.

Perhaps we could have a race!

Strange Rituals

"In the name of the Father, the Son and the Holy Ghost..."

What is that awful noise?

These English words rang out over the loudspeakers at sunrise and the older girls jumped out of bed, snatched their towels and began to line up at the door. Clearly we were meant to do the same so I, along with the other new girls, followed the example, stripping off our homemade nightclothes, grabbing our towels, tying them below our shoulders and lining up at the door. Though I had no idea what was being said, I was at least able to recognize that we were been told to wake up – as if I could sleep through such a racket.

The sound of a gong and the voice of a nun still rings in my head when I think of my years at the Sacred Heart Girls

School. The morning prayers were signalled by the sound of a nun ringing a gong and then reciting the Lord's Prayer and the Hail Mary, Full of Grace prayer. This was followed by a chorus of young voices from the five dormitories repeating, after the nun, the memorized prayers.

The prayers made little sense to me. However, every morning I would eagerly await, hoping that instead of the nun's voice, it would be my mother's voice giving thanks to her Creator. But that never happened. The nuns were saying prayers in English, followed by an interpreter's voice in Kiembu.

My routine while growing up in the village was different. Mother would say prayers in Kiembu, our language. She would thank the Creator for giving us another day and ask blessings for the day. She would always ask for guidance and protection for the seen and the unseen.

When my parents sent me to boarding school, they had no idea what they had done to this very valuable morning connection with my Creator, whom I had learned was mightier than anything imaginable, but whose presence was essential for our everyday living. However, in this new environment, I was exposed to a spiritual practice that revolved around a foreign god, language, images and procedures that made very little sense to a nine-year old girl.

After lining up at the door, a nun met us and gestured for us to follow. The older girls seemed to know what this was all about, but none of us young ones were brave enough to ask the obvious question.

Where were they taking us?

The nun led us out of our dorm, through the hallways to the steps down to the main level. We reached a door and I realized that we must be headed outside.

Were we going out to play?

Why would we need to bring our towels?

If one rule was clear, it was that we were not to talk. The younger nun, who seemed to do all the translating, had informed us that there was to be no talking. That was fine with me.

Who would I talk to, anyway?

We followed the small steps down to the concrete courtyard. I hazarded a look around, searching for any clues that would give me a better idea of what was going to happen next. There was a steel pipe suspended above the ground and a drain underneath the opening. It must be a pipe for water though I had never seen one arranged like that before.

What was all this about?

We made two lines in front of a long pipe. The first twenty girls in our line moved forward and stood opposite each other on either side of the pipe. This long pipe, which was about one-foot-high above the ground, had holes on either side and before I could connect my thoughts, one of the nuns turned a handle and water came gushing out, drenching them and sending shivers racing through their feet and faces. Remember, all of us were still wrapped in our towels.

How cold was the water?

Why were they still standing there?

It certainly didn't look pleasant.

The girls were given a moment to soap themselves before another gush of water descended upon them. Soap effectively washed away, the girls wraps their towels tightly around themselves, shivering, then walked in file back to their dormitory.

This was to be our daily bathing. I was not looking forward to the water pipe. Already, I missed the river and the water bowls. This drenching process was effective but looked horribly uncomfortable and my theory was confirmed when it was my turn under the pipe

Following what the other girls were doing, I selected my spot and waited for the nuns to turn on the water. Soaping myself became a nearly impossible task as my arms refused to extend. The chill took my breath away, forcibly tightening every muscle in my body and sent my teeth chattering immediately. Cold was not something I was used to tolerating and I preferred not to experience it again. But for the stern-faced nun silently pushing me to move faster lest I be doused with water before I was through, I would have given in to the stiffness and stood still until my body warmed again. Somehow I managed to complete the task, or perhaps I just ran out of time; the water rushed over me again and I at least had the presence of mind to rub at my skin to clear the soap.

Once bathing was complete, we all rushed back to our dorms, dressed quickly and lined up at the door to be walked to church. I wondered what kind of bathing did we really do when we had our towels around us? Maybe our faces, heads, hands, armpits and our legs?

Staying silent was a difficult task as I was so used to chatting with my friends and family as we walked from place to place. I occupied my busy mind by observing our path to the church, my classmates and especially the nuns that led us there. They were all so serious and I began to wonder where their families were, when they got to talk with their friends or what they did for fun. Perhaps I would ask later, once I had learnt English and could ask in their language.

We had arrived at the church if the ornate doors were any indication. The nuns opened the doors and we quietly filed into the largest room I had ever seen. The lights were incredible, glittering like stars. There were so many on the walls, hanging from the ceiling. My eyes were going all over the place and soon all I could see were images of people that didn't look like me at all, but like the pale nuns, all hanging on the walls.

I was delighted by the colours and wondered what each one meant.

Who were these people and ... ?

What was that?

There was a man, almost naked except for a cloth around his hips and he was hanging on a cross by his hands and feet.

Oh my God, why would they bring that to this place?

That was so depressing and miserable. It was so well lit and he was just hanging there ... why?

What did he do that he was hung there?

Still staring at this horrible sight, I followed the other girls to the front of the church and realized that each girl was kneeling down and making a strange motion with their hands before standing again and going to their seats. I studied their movements carefully as I was sure I was meant to do the same.

When it was my turn, I knelt down, facing the door that we entered from before standing and walking to my seat. Perhaps they would tell us what that was all for, later. When I sat down, I started, nearly standing again as the cold wood hurt my knees. The dress my sister made for me was very short and did nothing to protect my legs from the unforgiving benches. Knowing better than to ask for help; I settled into my seat and waited for the wood to warm.

The man at the front, dressed in strange robes, said many things in English and I listen intently as if paying attention would suddenly make the foreign words clear to me. Eventually, he finished and I was no closer to understanding the words than I was yesterday. We were told to stand and begin filing back out of the church once more. That morning ritual was so different from what I was used to.

Outside, in the hallway, we stopped and my name was called.

Oh no! What did I do?

I had just followed everyone else; surely there was no mistake in that?

Nearly all one hundred girls were standing in the hallway, waiting to go to their classrooms for the half hour study period before breakfast. Now everyone was going to be mad at me (so I thought) for the delay. They stared at me, knowing that I was in trouble. I wondered if any of them knew what I had done wrong and whether or not they would have warned me had we been allowed to talk.

Seeing no alternative, I walked to the front of the room where a big tall nun was standing and to her right was an older short nun. They both looked at me with hard eyes. The elderly nun spoke and the younger one translated.

"Catherine, you're very disrespectful in church."

Disrespectful?

I just followed what everyone else did.

"What did I do?" I replied, so confused and desperate to understand. This was not how my first day was supposed to go.

"You're kneeling with your back to the altar and showing your underwear to the priest."

No!

"What? What do you mean?"

"You have been kneeling down but you should not give your back to the altar."

"I didn't know!"

Oh my God.

I had been facing the wrong way when I knelt in church. How embarrassing! But the embarrassment and pain was soon doubled when the nun slapped me across the face in punishment for my error. Her fingers were very fat and the blow was so painful. I felt the sting on my skin and in my eyes. I fought to hold back the tears as they sent me back to the line and we silently made our way to our classroom. Apparently, my punishment was over, at least the physical part. And within a few minutes the bell rang and we all filed to the dining hall for breakfast, where the walls and roof were all corrugated iron.

Once in the hall, we were led to a table stacked high with metal cups and metal bowls. They made a horrible sound in the otherwise silent room as the porridge ladle hit the rims of the bowls. I took my portion along with a cup of water and made my way to a table with my classmates.

Someone was reading to us from a book and I was reminded of my midday readings with my mother. I wished I understood what they were reading to us. I wanted to know, but the language was beyond me. Once I learnt English, the first thing I would do was find that book they were reading from and reread everything I had missed. Perhaps my mother would like to hear these stories as well.

As I looked around the room, many of my year mates were staring at me. Suddenly I was grateful we were not allowed to talk because I would have asked them why they were looking at me. Was it because the big nun had slapped me so hard or was it because I had not started eating my breakfast. Oh well, I said to myself, I am sure one of these days, they will make a mistake and they will be slapped.

I had begun to tip the bowl of porridge to my lips when I saw something strange. Pulling back, I observed my meal and realized it was moving, and not because I was tipping the bowl. There were little bugs in the porridge, weevils, but I was too hungry to care. I knew the other girls had received the same porridge and no one had brought it to the attention of the nuns. This must be common.

I closed my eyes and ate, pretending all the while that I was in my mother's kitchen, with my mother's cooking, instead of this confusing and depressing place. The no taste of the porridge threatened to break apart my fantasy and I quickly took a sip of water to wash it away but even the water tasted strange. At least I was not hungry anymore.

A Life-Altering Smile in Class

Sister Carmen was a gentle woman; motherly and warm. She made an effort to welcome the students and she spoke my language so I loved to ask her questions. The memory of my first day in church still lingered and, though I had begun to learn English, much of Mass was still lost on me. The glittering of the candelabras enchanted me; I had never seen so much light inside a room not coming from the sun.

Still, the depressing images were a startling contrast to the brilliant room and I wanted to understand why they would put such miserable people in such a pretty space. Sister Carmen would often answer my questions if I had completed my studies and I had worked to ensure that once in a while I would get moments to ask her questions. On this particular day, I had completed our last assignment when I saw her walk past our classroom. I rushed to her, cleared my voice and said, "Sister, why would people be hanging in there, being stripped of clothes?"

And she said, "No, that's Jesus Christ, the son of God, who died for you."

"Died for me? For what? What did I do?"

"He died for your sins."

"What sins? What sins did I commit for somebody who didn't even know me, to die for me?" As a young child, I was moved and tried to figure out what I could have done that made someone be killed. Maybe the lie about my name. I promised myself to let the nuns know that I lied about my name. Hopefully, once this was cleared, I could revert to Njoki; I smiled to myself at the thought of being called Njoki.

Sister Carmen launched into a long explanation of how the son of God was sent for us and died for us. Her story seemed fantastic and I struggled to connect the information with something that was more familiar. To me, he felt like an ancestor. Back home, we remembered the ancestors from generations past and celebrated what they did for us, long before we were born. I made that observation to Sister Carmen and she thought for a moment before replying.

"Yes, if you want to call him that, you may. Just remember that this isn't God. This is the son of God who was sent to wipe your sins away once you accept him. Catherine, talk to Jesus sometime. He will listen to you and he will solve all your problems. You should consider being confirmed as a Christian."

"Confirmed? What do you mean confirmed?"

"Don't worry, Catherine. All this will make sense to you one day. For now, tell baby Jesus your needs."

Baby Jesus – why was the man on the cross called a baby? I thought to myself – he is not a baby! I decided to leave that for another day.

For the rest of the day – perhaps the rest of the week – I considered what I had learned. Ancestors were in the church. Some of them I did not even know I had. Learning that I had a family I didn't even know about warmed my heart and I began to feel more at home. I was not quite sure what she meant that God was not an ancestor, or maybe she meant that the statue in the church was not God.

This is really good, I thought. Someone who does not know me, a really old ancestor, could die for me so I could be forgiven.

I still had so many questions, but I had asked all I could for the day. I had learnt that the book they read to us during meals was called *The Book of Saints*. Our task was to listen to the stories of each of the saints and then reflect on their good deeds and how we might be like them. This was a heavy task and it took much of my time outside of my studies. I didn't want to fall behind so thanked Sister Carmen and ran back to class to study.

I began to enjoy church more and more after that. The stories were beginning to make sense and I enjoyed talking to God through our many prayers. The images on the wall and the man on the cross, Jesus Christ, were no longer so scary or depressing. They reminded me, every time I walked in church, that I had so much more to learn.

Our days were regimented. We woke up and prayed, washed and went to church, prayed and ate, prayed and did our studies, prayed at noon, studied again, prayed in the afternoon, played outside, prayed before dinner and then prayed before we went to bed. Prayer marked every transition from one activity to another.

In the beginning, I struggled to connect my parents' prayers to our Creator with the baby Jesus that the nuns talked about. What was Jesus like? Why did we pray to baby Jesus and the adult Jesus that I saw in the church? I was so confused. With my family, we would pray before every meal but not the way we prayed here. My mother and father would take care to remember everyone who joined us for dinner. They would ask how each person's day went, offer advice when needed and give thanks for any blessings.

Here, prayer was much more about asking for forgiveness and guidance. Hopefully, it would make more sense the more I learnt. But, to be honest, sometimes I missed praying to our Creator, Ngai, Mwene Nyaga because he seemed so much happier and gentle. The adult Jesus seemed so sad and I didn't know what to do. Perhaps I could ask Sister Carmen another day.

My constant exposure to English with the repetition through prayer, Mass and lessons made it easier for me to learn and soon I fell in love with the language and all that knowing it made available to me. I continued to make progress, laughing and playing every chance I got. School had become everything I'd ever dreamt it to be. I studied and learnt, and sometimes, I would even teach some of my classmates.

Some of them struggled and traded me things from home for completed homework assignments. I knew it was wrong to do their work for them, but I needed some of the things they had, like toothpaste, which I could not afford. Others I simply wanted, like sweet treats. I loved my school and the years went so fast. I had made good friends, I knew how to read and write in English and I could speak a few words of French.

I still remember to this day when Sister Joquim called my name – again – and asked me to step outside the study room. I was so scared. I thought I had done something wrong and I approached her shaking. Once outside, she asked me to follow her to the nuns' residence. Once inside, she gave me a bunch of flowers to take to the wife of the doctor in residence. It was her birthday, and her name was Catherine. I felt so special and important. In addition to that, the nun gave me a sweet to chew on my way to class. I was in seventh heaven. From there on, I knew I did not have to fear Sister Joquim.

This gave me courage to ask her about the lady in church who was holding a baby.

"Oh Catherine, Catherine, that's Mary, mother of Jesus, who is constantly praying for us sinners. I thought you learnt about this when you got baptized?"

"Baptized, Sister, what do you mean baptized?" I asked, stopping to look at the nun. What was she talking about? It was just then, I remembered. I had given myself a foreign name, yes, but I truly did not know these teachings. . . . I closed my eyes, and asked Jesus on the cross to forgive me and Mary, mother of baby Jesus, to pray for me.

I could not wait for the holidays to go home, to share with my brother and my friend Patricia all these new things I was learning. I also felt the need to take a break from this routine, and to be far from this place, but I would miss the prayers and the month-end retreats.

At the end of each month, there was a "retreat" beginning Friday night for all the girls. Everyone was absolutely silent, no talking aloud, and the silence lasted until Sunday evening. During this time, I spent every moment I could learning more about how to serve God. I spent lots of time talking to baby Jesus and to Saint Catherine and Saint Antonio.

Mary, the mother of Jesus, had become my second mother. I talked to her all the time and during these long silent weekends, I talked to her and I asked her to intercede for me. We were not allowed to do anything other than read, pray and reflect. I took each task seriously, determined to do it right. By the end of the year, I was sure that the only way to serve God was to become a nun, and that became my plan. I wondered what Mother would think of that. By the end of the first year, I was also fluently reading and speaking in English. This was so comforting for me as I had read many English novels and I wanted to share their stories with my mum.

On a light note, one nun gave us classes in Irish dance steps. I became very good at it and soon I was one of the few girls who was asked to perform during parents' day or any school events. The Irish dance became part of my life and when I left Sacred Heart Girls School and joined Kyeni Girls High School, which was across the street, I continued enjoying the dancing and many evenings I would gather other girls and I would teach them the steps.

This went on for almost a year in my new school, until that day when Ms. Simpson, the French teacher, interrupted our fun. I was so delighted with it all. Here I was, sitting with a group of girls that might not have otherwise ever spoken to me in the village. At school, we were all here to learn and play and dance, I could not be happier. The very thought brought a smile to my face and I laughed out loud for the fun of it ...

... and then Ms. Simpson walked in. The class went silent and I turned forward, a smile still stretching my face.

She looked right at me.

"Who has been making noise?"

I kept smiling. We'd all been making noise. What an odd question.

"Catherine, why are you smiling? What is so funny about being naughty and being without discipline?"

I sat back in my seat, shocked, and the smile fell from my face.

Had I really been so bad?

Was smiling so wrong?

Perhaps I had not been taking school as seriously as I should. After all, I was here to learn, second year in high school, earn my grades and get my diploma; nothing more. I considered my epiphany for the rest of the class before deciding that, yes, Ms. Simpson was quite right. I should be taking this much more seriously and, starting today, things were going to change.

It didn't take long for the other girls to notice. I no longer laughed or joked openly with my classmates. I was competitive and serious in class, answering questions every chance I got and spending all my free time studying and praying. My reading of novels enabled my spoken English to improve and I cherished the silence and the discipline that came with the reading habit. My smiles were rare and fleeting, often drowned out by the intensity of my focus and religious devotion.

A Moment of Reflection: From My Canadian Kitchen to Kenya

Teaching has been taking a great deal of my time and attention and I have to admit that my housekeeping has gotten a bit out of control. Today, this fine Saturday, I've decided to do some serious cleaning, starting with my kitchen.

It's impossible to keep a kitchen clean for long since, as soon as you've cleaned it, it's time to use it again. Even looking at it right now makes my limbs heavy and my mind long for a book to read instead. Fortunately, laziness was long ago trained out of me by Italian and Irish nuns, cold water pipes, rigorous prayer and rigid structure.

Perhaps I'll start with the easy part and wash the dishes. As I approach the sink, I can't help but smile, as the very concept of running water that turns hot or cold at the twist of a handle simply delights me. Kijiji had no such luxuries and as a young girl I would have considered such a thing pure magic. I turn the handle simply to feel the water change temperature without the aid of an open fire or large pot to heat it in.

Even the sponge I hold is a novelty compared to the sisal strings or the sand from the river that we used to wash our pots with. Liquid soap has brought me much entertainment with its foam and the little bubbles that escape and float around each time I squeeze the bottle too fast. I fill one side of the sink with soapy hot water and the other side with cold clear water, practising the hygiene that I learned long ago from my mother. Today, as I stand in front of the sink, I have a choice; I can either put all the dirty dishes in a dishwasher on my right or just use this time to reflect as I clean the utensils. I choose the latter. How strange it is to think that at one time, we would wash our pots in river water drawn from crocodile-infested waters.

I wonder what my children would think if I shared my rural upbringing. Maybe I should. This may teach them not to waste water or resources.

Even my dishes evoke a sharp contrasting memory of steel bowls and cups issued to us at the Sacred Heart Girls School. Each time I use these dishes I appreciate their soft sounds rather than the harsh clang of metal on metal that accompanied many meals in my youth.

Dishes washed and dried, I move to the countertops and start wiping down the surfaces with a soapy sponge. The motion is easy and soothing and so very different from the stone, clay or wooden surfaces that permeated my parents' house. Next in the cleaning line comes the coffee maker – the latest model, Keurig, where I can press the button and have a fresh cup of coffee or tea. There are also my different models of blenders and a collection of Tupperware that seems to grow every day.

How could it be that I've come to own so much stuff? I cannot help it – tears start to well when I remember how from mother-back I had a longing to have everything in the Indian shop. We had so little at home, yet we had everything. Here in my home in Toronto, I have so much, yet I want more, I am thinking of buying a new stove, fridge, dishwasher…my house is bursting with stuff hanging from everywhere. And today, I feel like I am the Indian market – I have so much stuff that I do not even know what to do with it all.

We never needed all of this at home.

Why do I need it now?

Is life so different in Canada that it requires a kitchen full of things to keep up with the demands of the Western lifestyle?

It would appear so because the very idea of throwing out any of these silly bits brings on a panic that sets my heart racing. I soothe myself for a moment by reorganizing my collection, separating and arranging the lids by size and placing smaller bowls inside larger ones to save space.

The toaster is another modern marvel. To the younger me, this would have been a three-stone fireplace that burned anything placed on it while leaving it still edible. Even more wonderful is the microwave, the refrigerator and the oven. While the concept of an oven or a fridge is not so strange, and I had used them in Nairobi before moving to Canada, in the village, all that we had was that three-stone fireplace and our ceiling was our storage. Even the idea of cooking one meal at a time rather than large quantities of things that would last for days is a novelty.

I wonder what my late friend Patricia or my mother would think now if they saw the house I live in and all the wonders that technology has created. So many things that would take us all day have been transformed into a minute's worth of work. Drawing water from the river, harvesting fruits and coffee from the fields and walking to the market have been reduced and refined. Now I turn on the faucet, open the refrigerator or pantry door or drive to the grocery store.

There are so many people I would love to show this life to – and in particular Patricia, who had passed away without explanation. She would have loved to play with all these little gadgets and I can only guess how many hours we would spend running around the parks, stores and play-grounds marvelling at the world and all it has become in so short a time.

As a child, my imagination would run wild; creating things out of air, dirt and plants that I thought would never really be possible. Now, I sit in my kitchen, in my house in Canada, staring at the products of my imagination, realizing that I wasn't the only one who thought of such things. In fact, someone imagined them and then figured out how to make them real.

I envy that kind of ingenuity at times. What a joy it would be to have the knowledge and wherewithal to imagine a device that would heat food in a box, freeze things forever or even just suck the dirt from a carpet and keep it from falling back down. My talents clearly lay in other avenues, and there are times when I wonder what else I've imagined that someone else has thought of and ventured to create.

Patricia would have loved all these just as much as the late Muikaria. She was a couple of months younger than us and as eager to learn as I was. I think of her often and miss her dearly. She died while giving birth many years ago. I've left so much behind in Kenya, but all my memories of that country are intact in my subconscious. It is strange how my dreams take me back to my village and what was familiar to me while growing up, while Canada, my home for over thirty years, also becomes part of my dream world. Coming to Canada to further my education was supposed to be a temporary move. But the move became a permanent one, although it's fluid both temporally and physically because I am constantly moving between the two continents. Frequent visits to Kenya help me stay connected, but I often wish I could bring more of Kenya back with me to Canada. At the entrance of my home is a piece of art from Kenya. The wall of my staircase is lined with art from the continent.

Perhaps much of my home is already here in my kitchen. Each of these objects serves to remind me of a moment spent dreaming with the ones I love. They don't have to be relics of times passed. Instead, I can choose to see them as symbols of accomplished goals and completed dreams. They hold and evoke memories of hours spent playing, laughing and fantasizing about a world much more complex and mysterious than the one we lived in at the time.

Like many, I have lost friends and family along the way. I've made seemingly bad choices that have worked out in my favour and seemingly good choices that cost me too much. Yet, somehow, all of that has led me here and I cannot regret it.

My Mother's Footprints

Dear Mama,

Thirty years ago, I boarded a plane headed to North America to study; acquire books and experiential knowledge, more degrees; and hopefully, quench my spirit for adventure. Something was pushing me to seek the real lifestyle of other countries and other people. Despite the fact that I had travelled to Europe for holidays, there was something else I was seeking for. I was not sure what. I had a good life, I had lots of material wealth, I had two university degrees, what on earth was I longing for? Was I being pushed out of my comfort zone to awaken my African spiritual being? Was it to awaken my dormant ancestral knowledge that had been submerged or subsumed in my

Western lifestyle? But I was in Africa, and as far as I knew, Africa had nothing to offer me. How wrong I was. At this particular time in my life, I had no idea that Africa lived in me. Looking back, on that cold night on August in 1987, I cannot help but feel that it was a moment of disruption of my routine, it was a moment of awakening. Although, on that night, I was truly sad.

With tears welling in my eyes, I left Africa for further studies. Our relatives travelled from Embu and different parts of Nairobi to come and say goodbye. Someone rented a vehicle to bring as many people as possible from the village – people who were carrying my dad's blessings (in terms of Kenyan shillings and travel blessings) as he was too old to travel. Their mission was to report to Dad in detail how I looked and to take back to him my gifts to him. Yes, the memories of that night are very vivid as I said goodbye to my husband, my son and two daughters, my brothers and sisters, nieces, nephews, cousins and friends and their families.

I've only just begun to realize that this move has changed my life forever and I want to share with you what I've learned.

The first time I realized this move was a life-altering move I had just arrived in my new city, Fredericton, New Brunswick, and glanced into a mirror. There, facing me, was *you*. Not my face but your face, Mama. I nearly shouted, "Oh my God, what is this? Why has my face altered? Why do I look like my mother?"

Your face, young and youthful and full of promise, was frightening, but reassuring. You are one of my guiding spirits. You had travelled with me and would be with me in this place where I had no relatives or friends.

The second time came when I realized that North America was *not* paved with gold! There were people in the streets asking for money! Yes! *Begging* for money, while others were homeless. How can this be? Not in a Western country where all the wealth, education, everything good came from. What a bitter pill to swallow!

The third was my social class. I grew up in the countryside with little material wealth, but my husband's acquired social class had become *my* class and I was considered to be well off. But here, in my new country, my social class was shattered. I was nobody. My husband's money, cars and property had no weight in this country. All that they knew of me was what they could see: a Black African woman student, someone in need of rescue because she could hardly speak English!

Can you believe it, Mama, when I used to read English novels and then translate the stories for you?! According to many here, my English is *incomprehensible*. I thought I had mastered the English language with the many English novels and literary works I have read. Apparently, this was not written on my forehead and despite having a master's degree, it was not good enough to be admitted to my master's degree program! *I* was not good enough. Fortunately, Mama, I was able to argue my case and my conditional admission was revoked. I started my degree without having to write qualifying exams or major papers.

The fourth time was when I realized that I was not only African, but Black, and one who spoke with an African accent, Mama. Of course, I know I am from the continent of Africa. What I did not know was that I am Black and people *care* about that. The colour of my skin means something to people in this side of the world, Mama! You know something, I will research this issue, and next time you visit me, I will have an answer for you. It's like there's a story written on my skin that I am not allowed to read.

Mama, it has taken me more than two years to make sense of the colour of my skin. When I completed my master's degree, I thought I could work for a couple of months before I decided what to do next. I applied for a work permit to teach in a college. I was informed that I did not have teaching experience. I indicated to the immigration officer that I am a trained teacher and I had been teaching at one of the universities in Kenya. I was told, unfortunately, I did not have Canadian experience.

A week later, I went back to the same officer to inform her that I had found a job as a chambermaid (Mama, this is a glorified title for a cleaner of hotel rooms). Listen to this, Mama, there were no questions asked, I was issued with a one-year work permit. I thanked the lady for the permit, but then I asked her whether I could use the same document to teach. She called my name out loud and said, "Njoki, do you know how to read? What does the document say?" At that moment I opened the envelope and unfolded the document and it was clearly indicated in black and white, I could only work as a chambermaid. Mama, two master's degree, and a diploma in business studies, and all that I was allowed to do was to clean other people's ... Mama, I was devastated. I cried, I begged the lady to change the document and she looked at me and said I had taken too much time and I should leave her office.

Since that moment, Mama, I have become aware of race issues and the fact that one's race and sometimes other identity markers dictate how business is carried out. This particular realization opened my eyes! All of a sudden, I saw the divide. I had woken to a world of division.

However, your spirit has become my constant companion. Your voice is so constant in my ears that I've even worried that I'm going crazy! But there is no craziness in your whispers, only reassurance. You say to me, "Do not be stuck on all these classifications! You are a child of our Creator, our Ngai, and in the eyes of our Creator, there is no race, gender, class, age or continent of birth. These labels are people's creations, Njoki. Never forget that."

My pen was my sword; I see that now. With this sword, if I master it well, I will open many doors not only for me but for many who have not come to understand how the world is governed, dominated, maintained and sustained. Your spirit enables me to navigate and simplify the complex matrix I find myself in. You have lived in me. I have read for you over and over again, I have written for you, plowed the world of academia with you.

Mama, as I start this renewed, energized life – do not leave me also tell Daddy that I need him more than ever – his wisdom, creativity, courage. I know the two of you have always been with me because the seeds you planted in me of honesty, sincerity, hard work, responsibility and resiliency are about to be regerminated. My dear parents, the climb in front of me is very steep and slippery, but I know you have given me the armour, and different ways of reminding me that my ancestors are with me. My Creator holds me high up when the path is too slippery to walk and when the road signs are not visible. There are grips to hold on to so that I can take my breath to seek clarity.

My Creator, the Ngai of my parents, sends me the guides to lead me so that I can deal with any obstacles and barriers that I may find on my path. Mama, Papa, you are in the spirit world and can see what we cannot. Remove all those clouds and crowds that blur my vision. I know I have a mission to accomplish. My Ngai, send me a guide to assist me to fulfill my purpose in life, to achieve my dreams and to acquire what is rightfully mine.

Keep me centred and focused, Lord. Help me to ritualize my life, so that each morning I start my day with renewed energy, vigour and focus. Let me produce the best that there is; let me be a good child, parent, nana, wife, sister, aunt, cousin, friend and colleague. Let me utilize my God-given gifts and, in particular, my creativity and imaginative thinking to make this world a better world, a place to live and love – not a cutthroat world of deceit and trickery.

Canada: My New Home

Dear Mama,

I love sharing my stories with you. I have more to tell you about this new place that you have accompanied me to. Please find a comfortable place and I will tell you more about my initial experiences in my new country. A country that has become a home not only for me but my children and their children.

Mama, okay.

I have so many experiences to share about my new home from my first week in Canada to the last couple of weeks after having been here for over three decades. I knew of Canada in my grade four class when our geography teacher asked us to board his imaginary vehicle as we travelled to Canada to visit the lumbering industry and the wheat-growing prairies. Mama, you may not remember, but I shared that story with you. And I still remember you telling me that one day I will have wings to fly and I will visit that faraway land.

I still remember my longing then to visit this strange place that had so much wood and grassland – that I later came to learn was wheat. I wondered why the teacher never talked about the people or even the land itself. I wondered whether the land had mountains, buildings and big rivers like we did. Who were the farmers? Did the people look like Mama or Baba? Did they use hoes to dig the land?

Mama, when it was time to fly to that place, you were no longer with us. You had left for the spirit world two years earlier. But I knew you were in the bus that brought the many people from the village to say goodbye to me.

Mama, do you remember, it was mid-August 1987, while flying over Canada for the first time, and I looked down from the window just before we landed, and all that I saw was mushy land with shrubs and bushes and many ponds. I wondered where all the trees and the wheat land that I had read about in books and the teacher had talked about were. What was interesting was that, as I looked out, I knew this would be my second home. Please do not ask me why. I don't have an answer. But I knew it would be the case. I was among a group of students who had attained a scholarship from Canadian International Development Agency (CIDA) to pursue graduate studies in Canada.

The orientation week was loaded with information and by the end of the week I felt so foreign, from the food, the everyday terminologies, the mall, but most confusing of all was the fact that people drove from the left-hand side of the car. I stored as much as I could and thought that once I got to my university, I would reflect on it and decide what made sense to me.

At the end of the week, I was driven to the airport and sent to the University of New Brunswick, on the east coast of Canada. Upon arrival there, I was welcomed by two students who helped me to settle in. I wish I could remember their names. They took me to the bank to open my first account with Royal Bank; then to the housing office to check on accommodation; then to a couple of thrift stores (I did not know at that time what these were); advised me how to go about changing my conditional acceptance to regular acceptance. By the end of the week I had found a place to stay, managed to remove the conditional acceptance for my master's degree, been matched with a host family from a nearby church, bought winter clothes from a thrift store and been given an office that I was to share with another graduate student from Kenya. All in all, I was ready for my twelve months of study before I could go home to see my family.

Mama, Canadians are great people, very polite and they smile a lot (I could be stereotyping a little). However, my initial housing arrangement was so difficult that I wanted to run as fast as I could and return to Kenya to my beautiful big home. I had rented a bedroom, very small, but cozy, in the house of a lady who had a dog. What made me uncomfortable was the fact that the dog shared the house with us and was bathed in the same bathtub. Although I had a couple of dogs in Kenya, they slept in their own kennel, outside, and the gardener sprayed them with water whenever they needed a bath. I gave notice and left. That was a huge conflict of traditions.

The great thing was, Mama, people were very helpful and understanding and within less than a week, I had found another place to stay. This time, I got a room in a basement apartment that had five students. What shocked me was when I went to see the place and the landlady opened a door that led below to somewhere – I had never been to a basement before, nor did I know that people lived in basements. In Kenya, basements were mainly found in office buildings and they were only used for parking cars. However, I had very little choice by now, and I accepted the accommodation and settled in for the semester. It is important to note that this was the place where, during my first week there, that you came to visit me, Mama. You appeared on my mirror – you looked at me and I knew from there on, you were beside me. Thank you, Mama.

It has been a long road to travel, from that room in the basement to my current four-bedroom home with a basement. In between those two places, I met professors and laypeople who were extremely good to me and assisted me in so many ways. Many took me in when I had no place to stay in between rentals, others were willing to write letters for me to attain more scholarships to pursue my Ph.D. Others gave me a car, clothes, you name it.

What amazed me was how some professors thought I knew nothing at all because I spoke English with a different accent. I still remember in some instances I would ask a question and the professor would just move on as if I hadn't spoken. Or I would put my hand up and I would be totally ignored. Due to my newness in Canada, I could not make sense of the professors' indifference and when I shared my experiences with other racialized students they told me it was discrimination.

"What do you mean discrimination?" I asked.

One person said, "You have not seen it yet?"

"Prepare yourself for the worst."

"You were lucky when you were looking for a place to stay, we assisted you. Some of us who came earlier were turned down so many times. Don't get me wrong, our land-lady, she is Caucasian, but really good. She has made us all very comfortable. Look at how she took you in and gave you an ensuite bedroom – yes, it is very small, and yes, we all live in the basement, but still, she is a wonderful human being."

"There is something else," I continued. "Why do people refuse to sit near me in church? I always find myself all alone on a bench. And ... eh ... and when I try to shake hands with others, they keep their hands to their sides ... Why? I am a bit confused."

Since those few months in Canada, I have learnt so much. I have learnt the discourse of race, its interlocking systems of domination. I have written on issues of discrimination and have given many talks on the subject. I have learnt not to be a victim. I decided at some point not to spend so much energy analyzing why so-and-so was mean to me, or why I was denied entry to this place or why some assumed my students were the professors and not me just because they were Caucasian. I have witnessed many discriminatory tendencies even from people whom I thought knew better. Many Canadian (from different races – Black, Asian, Caucasian, etc.) have asked me really stupid questions such as "You must be lucky to be here – Africa is so hot" or "Where did you learn to speak English?" or "When do you plan to return back to Africa?" or "Do you live in the capital of Africa or in the rural area?" Hey, Africa is a continent; it has fifty-three countries that were a result of the Scramble for Africa during the Berlin Conference when the continent was chopped into different segments depending on which European countries were seated at the table.

Mama, sometimes I get tired answering all these questions. Sometimes I get depressed when I am denied my rights, when my pay raise is different from other colleagues of mine despite the fact I work so hard – Mama, you told me to master the little figures that jump out of a page. I have done it, Mama, but I still find not everyone recognizes that. What I do know, Mama: I should always have a positive outlook and when I really need to chat, you are beside me.

Brothers' and Sisters' Gifts

The sisters made an announcement that in one month we were going on a school trip to Nairobi. I was in grade seven, thirteen years old, and I had never been to the city before. I was ecstatic. It was only later when they told us it would cost one hundred shillings that I realized I would not be able to go. I could not afford that kind of money.

The idea of being left behind while the rest of the girls travelled to the city was nearly too much. That night, I wrote to my parents and mentioned the trip, but I knew there was nothing to be done for it. I did my best to sound at peace with staying behind, not wanting them to think I was ungrateful.

When my older brother Njuki delivered something to the school two weeks before our trip I could not imagine what he might have brought me. He could not stay long, but I did my best to welcome him, told him of my studies and thanked him for visiting. Just before he left, he turned to me and said, "Sis, this package is for you. It's not fair for you to be left behind while the others go to the city."

I looked down at the small bundle, began to realize what was inside.

"Njuki, this is too much. I cannot take it."

"Yes, you can, and you will. Your path is in school and I want you to go on this trip. Take the money and learn."

I nodded my head with tears threatening to fall. In the bundle was one hundred shillings; enough to cover the cost of transportation over the two-hundred-kilometre distance to Nairobi, food and some pocket money. I couldn't quite believe what Njuki had done for me, but I was determined to pay him back. Someday, I would give him this money back, ten times over. He would never regret giving me this money.

Two weeks later, we all piled onto the bus for Nairobi, a small bit of money in our pockets, holding sandwiches made of bread and little else. There were so many of us squashed into each seat that the jostling of the bus over the uneven terrain made us knock into each other like reeds being pushed around by the wind. We sang Christian songs, prayed – of course we prayed – and chattered all the way to the city. The drive was simply wondrous and I spent most of my time staring intently out the window, desperate to see all that was on display.

I had no idea how big our country was! Just as I had decided that I never wanted our journey to end, I caught a glimpse of something off in the distance. It must be Nairobi.

What other concrete city would be out here?

I squirmed in my seat from sheer excitement, forgetting about my obsession with the landscape and becoming wholly devoted to exploring every bit of this monstrous city that I could possibly get to in our meagre time frame. My head was already swivelling from street end to street end as we disembarked from the bus. I saw street vendors peddling their wares, busy business people scurrying from sidewalk to sidewalk and a massive cathedral in the distance. It must be larger than our entire school. I knew it must be on our list of places to visit today and I couldn't wait to get started.

The nuns announced to us all the places we would be visiting. As I suspected, the cathedral was at the top of the list. But even more exciting was their declaration that we would be visiting the Library of Nairobi.

Oh my God, what fun!

When I am older, I thought, I will travel all the time, I just know it. And, I won't be restricted by any nuns. I'll travel on my own terms, explore the world and see all kinds of beautiful and fascinating things. But for now, I trotted behind the nuns, keeping up with the group and doing my best to memorize every detail of this majestic place.

Someone raced by me, a tall woman, and I heard *clack, clack, clack* as she moved down the street.

What is that?

I looked at her, trying to determine where the noise was coming from. Just as she was about to turn a corner,

I looked down at her feet. She was wearing high-heeled shoes. That was where the strange noise was coming from.

How can she move so quickly on those tiny little spikes? How does she not fall or slip?

I looked down at my own slippered feet and wondered if I would ever have a pair of shoes like that. I wanted to, but I simply could not imagine navigating the streets of Nairobi with so little to place my foot on. It was of no consequence that day. I had no shoes and I had places to go.

The cathedral was as big as I'd suspected, with glittering stained glass windows, massive statues and paintings, cavernous rooms and impossibly high ceilings. But, to be honest, the Library of Nairobi was even better. I was immediately enchanted by the quiet atmosphere and the temptation I felt to settle down on the floor and read everything I could get my hands on.

I would live here someday, I promised myself, this will be my favourite place to go and I will learn many things to share with my friends and family. Once again, I was desperately grateful for Njuki's extremely generous gift to me. He had done more for me at that moment than he would ever know and I would be forever indebted to him.

This was not the first or the last time one of my brothers would visit me at school with a gift I would be grateful for.

The three years I was in primary school, I did without shoes. My slippers were all that I came with; shoes were an expense my parents could not afford. The other girls teased me and I did my best to hide my embarrassment, knowing it would only make things worse. Focusing on studies and prayers was a shield against my darker emotions and I took care not to bring my worries home to my family.

So, of course, it came as an incredible surprise when my brother Mugeni arrived at Kyieni Girls High School and delivered to me a pair of new shoes. I was in grade nine. I could barely contain my excitement, both for his visit and for the wondrous gift of shoes. No more swishing down the hallways in my slippers, no more teasing, no more sideways glances at my feet.

I hugged Mugeni tightly before he left, desperate to express my gratitude at the expense he'd gone to and what he'd done for me. An overwhelming sense of love rushed through me as I remembered my family, my home and how much I had left behind to attend high school

A shout knocked me from my reverie and I realized that it was nearly time to go back to our dorms.

Perfect.

I could open my package in my bed and take my time appreciating my gift. Perhaps I would have time to write a letter home if I was diligent in my studies and finished early. Such letters were common in our first few weeks of school but now were a rare opportunity given our schedules and the availability of supplies.

After our evening prayer, I changed into my nightclothes quickly and settled down on my bed. I took a moment to revel in the mismatched wood planks that we used as beds and pulled my blanket up.

I ignored the questioning glances of the other girls. We were near our bedtime and no talking was permitted so there was no pressure on me to answer their silent questions.

I unwrapped the precious package, eager to see what my brother had chosen for me.

The lid slid off and fell to the blankets and I caught my first glimpse of a shiny object. Peeling back the wrapping, I unveiled a beautiful pair of beige high-heeled shoes. The material was smooth and I could see a faint reflection of the room in the surface. The shoes were simply beautiful. Pulling them out and placing the box on the floor with the utmost care, I simply could wait to try them on.

I slid one foot out from under the covers, eager to tie the laces and see if I could get away with walking around the room. Two feet on the floor and shoes to each side, I carefully lifted my feet and slid them into the shoes. How easy!

Sparing a glance around the room, I saw that I had lost the interest of the other girls and was reasonably sure I could walk for a short distance before someone made a comment. I stood, allowing my blankets to fall back on the bed, and prepared to take my first step. The high heel was awkward, but I was determined to learn to walk steadily like the other girls.

I raised my foot from the ground and was just about to take that step when I felt a funny sensation. The shoe was moving, even though I was not. What was this? I put my foot down, repositioned myself and made another attempt. The same sensation. I looked down and in the last bit of candlelight I could see my foot pressed into the front of the shoe and a large gap at my heel. No!

I sat down in a heap. How could this be?

The shoes were too big and I could not wear them.

The weight of disappointment made my body sag. I was so certain . . . anger quickly erupted and I thought of Mugeni and his carelessness. How could he buy me shoes and not even bother to find out if they would fit?

No, Njoki.

No.

This was not the way. I was disappointed, but not angry at my brother. He had done a very generous thing for me and it was up to me to make the best of it. The next day, I shoved newspapers into the toes of my new shoes, determined to make them fit. After I got used to the feeling of my toes being crushed by the paper, I began to move more smoothly and took delight in the *clack, clack, clack* that my new shoes made as I walked down the concrete hallway.

After a week, I had learnt to walk in the shoes and no one knew that I had paper shoved in the toes to make them fit. I walked with pride; a pride I shared with my brother, my family. I had been given a gift by my brother and I would do everything I could to repay him.

The generosity of my brothers and sisters was limitless. I will never forget when Anthony, my late brother, visited me with his wife, Mary. This time, my brother, who had gotten his first teaching job, brought me a jar of Nivea cream. This was a novelty in itself. A cream, and a beauty cream. Wahoo – what else could I want? I did not have to walk around with my ashy face and legs. Every morning, I would put on my cream and smell so good. As if that was not enough, brother Anthony took me to Nairobi (this was my second visit) to have my eyes checked. I will never, ever forget the place he took me for lunch. Someone was there singing from what I thought was a box, which I found out later was a television set. Many years later, I saw the same singer and I found out that he was Nat King Cole. I have most of his songs in my collection because that first experience of seeing him sing became part of my unforgettable experience.

My sister Mary was a domestic science teacher, and I tell you, I truly benefited from her profession. Whenever she made dresses for her girls – Cecilia, Lucy, Cathy and Maggi – she would always include me. I felt special and I truly treasured those dresses, one of which I was wearing when I stole the show from my brother Henry, who had invited a photographer to our home to take some snapshots. I quickly ran behind him and became part of the treasured moments. At the time of taking the photograph, he did not know I was in it until the photographer brought the photo. My brother was mad, but I was thrilled, because that was my first photograph. It was one of those mischievous things I had done, which I never regretted. From that moment until his death, we had a special bond. Henry, may your soul rest in peace.

Gratitude: The Gifts and Giving

The Canadian malls are not necessarily my favourite places, but I do appreciate the convenience of being able to get so much done in one place. Malls remind me of the bustling streets of Nairobi or the market my mother used to take me to as a young girl. I will be flying back home soon to visit my family and need a few provisions and gifts to take along on this journey.

Right now, I am looking for shoes. I've developed a fondness for shoes though I can't say I am a collector like some. I am especially partial to pairs of beige high-heeled shoes that shine in the sunlight and go *clack, clack, clack* on the floor and walkways.

Just after moving to Ontario, I discovered a little shoe store in the corner of the Eaton Centre that always caught my eye with its colourful wares and ever-changing stock. Walking around the university grounds is hard on my footwear and I found myself in this little shoe store far more often than I ever expected.

The girls all came to know me by name and now even anticipate when I might be due for another visit. I love the warmth I feel when I walk in, hearing my name in greeting and how I am immediately directed to some of the new options that might appeal to me.

Who knew such a luxury would be mine someday?

Who knew I would be living in my own home where I could do whatever I wanted, such as buy a pair of high heels that would fit me perfectly every month, and smile every time I put them on. I walked around the streets of Toronto for days in my new shoes, learning to balance on their precarious points and enjoying the *clack, clack, clack* they made on the asphalt. One thing I did not anticipate was the horrible blisters on the balls of my feet and my heels from the strange shape of the shoe. It took me a few weeks to recover from my first few days of exploration.

On this particular trip back home, I'll also be visiting Njuki and his family. Since the day he brought me one hundred shillings to pay for my first trip to Nairobi, I've dreamed of the time that I would be able to repay him for his generosity.

After I graduated from the University of Toronto with my Ph.D., I felt it was important for me to say thank you to my brother Njuki, who had paid for that school trip for me in the late sixties. I was well aware that the value of his gift was far more than the monetary value of the package.

One hundred shillings in the late sixties was almost equivalent to 150 Canadian dollars then and was a great deal of money for my brother to spare. But, much more valuable was the experience and wonders that money purchased for me. After experiencing the city, I knew that travel, knowledge and exploration must forever be a part of my life and I've done everything I can since then to make sure I have these things.

The first time I was able to bring some money back to Njuki, I was so happy and proud to be in a position to share with my family. Finally, I was able to repay him just a small piece of the joy he brought me through his generosity.

"Njuki," I said to him, "you'll never truly know what you did for me that day. You gave me such an incredible gift and it allowed me to experience so much. I remember that trip so vividly and still feel so much inspiration from what I saw. You'll never know, but I do want to say thank you for your generosity. I may never be able to match what you've given me, but I can try."

I handed Njuki a package containing ten thousand shillings. I was so proud to be able to give this to him. This exchange was about so much more than money. Because of him and the rest of my family, I had become successful enough to bring money and wisdom back to the next generation. I could share with them some of the resources that had come to me because of my education and experiences.

From travelling around the world with my husband Mike to moving to Canada to go to school and then teach, I have made sure to reach far beyond the borders of Kenya. And still, when it is time to go home and rest, it is always

Kenya I think of, with my brothers, nieces, nephews and all the memories and ancestors that country holds for me.

Even though most of the kijiji is gone – only a few members of my family still remain there, my brother Anthony's wife and Kathani's second wife, as well as my parents' graves – I still feel connected to my country, my rural upbringing.

When I was about three or four years old, everyone in the village was evacuated by the militia. The residents were transported to an "alternative settlement," which was really a small camp for the purpose of making sure the Ena people would be safe.

Because I was so small and my mother could not handle two small children – my youngest brother was about a year old and still a baby – my brothers, Henry, Njagi, Njuki and Mugeni, took me to their school. I stayed at Ena Primary School with them and visited my mother's camp once a week. My dad was away from home and he could not be of much help to my mum then. I do not remember how long this went on – maybe a couple of months – but less than a year – but we returned home and soon after that, Kenya attained her political independence in 1963.

Nairobi still inspires me as well. Its cultural significance and symbolism of progress and abundance reminds me of what is possible when people strive to grow and learn. The library there is still one of my favourite places to visit and I still much prefer the quiet reading rooms to the cavernous and imposing cathedral I once visited with my classmates.

Now I was visiting Kenya to see my family and share with them my success and happiness. Njuki's daughter wants to go to university for her master's degree and I have offered to support her efforts emotionally as well as spiritually. After some hard work and planning, I am now able to support her with some money and I was going to let Njuki know about the offer once I arrived.

The anticipation of being able to share this gift with them made me impatient to leave. My flight was in two more days and I was nearly ready to go. Working for the university here in Canada allows me the flexibility to make such trips on a somewhat regular basis and I jump at every opportunity to explore the world in all the ways I had dreamed of as a child.

Finally, I arrive at my shoe shop and I cannot help but feel grateful again that I can afford to buy shoes that fit me. I look around the mall, and there is so much glitter, the lighting is out of this world. The beauty of the mall makes me wonder whether one day, my kijiji will have a mall like this and if that happens, what will happen to the fields, the greencries and the people?

My Husband, the Maasai Man

I meet Michael, a Maasai, at my brother Mugeni's wedding. Later I found out that he was my brother's roommate at the university and that he was studying economics. I had no idea what economics was, but I knew immediately that I was in love with the man. He was warm and gentle. My heart raced when I was near him and when he left for Nairobi and I was left in the village, my heart was broken. Michael did not know that I loved him and that I wanted to be his wife – despite the fact that I had not completed high school at the time.

Almost two years later, I met Michael again, this time in my sister's house in Nairobi. I was mesmerized by him. While I knew I was supposed to be going to university, I was determined to get to know this man. After a few months of meeting in secrecy, Mike proposed. Saying yes was the easy part.

Going home and telling my mother that I was not going to university because I was getting married was a task I would rather not have completed. To calm my nerves on the drive to my mother's house, we talked of all the resorts we would visit in Kenya and the places in Europe we would go on holiday. I knew his words were true and, later, I would have pictures and souvenirs from each of the places he promised to take me.

Still, the task of telling my mother needed to be completed and, as we sat at my mother's kitchen table, I could barely look her in the eyes as I admitted to her that I would not be completing my education. In fact, I would be moving in with Mike at his home in Nairobi after today. I know I mumbled the words, barely strong enough to tell her at all. Her silence was terrifying.

What was interesting was the calm with which my dad received the information. He did not even ask for dowry. He turned to Mike and said that all he wanted was a bill of twenty shillings – that is equivalent to two dollars in today's currency – and a Land Rover to take him around. My brothers were upset, but there was nothing they could do to my dad. When a girl is getting married, the family of the bridegroom is supposed to give money, or cows, or goats. My father did not want anything of the sort. My brothers had written down a list of what they wanted, and my parents told them to keep their list in their pockets. But the exchange of gifts in form of dowry is very important, and in 2014, I called all my brothers together and gave each one of them a monetary gift. It was not much, but it was a token of appreciation and completion of the unpaid dowry.

After weeks of floating on the joy of wonders of marriage, I felt my world crashing down around me. I began to realize how deeply disappointed my mother was. Everything she had wanted for me, the freedom, the education and economic independence, had all stopped, at least in her eyes. She could barely look at Mike, and I wondered if she would ever forgive him, or me.

Mike explained to her that he would pay for me to go back to school and complete my education and even attain multiple degrees. Of course, at that time, I did not even understand what he meant by multiple degrees. But I knew he was telling the truth and it warmed my heart that he would attempt this appeal to my mother. She didn't seem to hear him though and stared at me without saying a word. Eventually, we had nothing more to say, and stood to leave.

I began to doubt myself. All that I had wanted to be was a professor, but now, without completing my education, I saw my dream thrown through the window. Why would I sacrifice my dream for marriage? What was attracting me to this man – was it his material wealth or was I genuinely in love? Did I really know what all this meant?

I had never left my home without giving my mother a good handshake as a form of goodbye, but at that moment, I was not sure that the gesture would have been welcome.

I supposed it didn't help the situation that Mike drove me to my home, through the dusty main street of Ena, in one of the latest Renaults. As we were about to leave for Nairobi, Mike looked at me and said, "On your wedding day, I will drive you from here in a Mercedes." It could just as easily have been a Volvo, an Audi or a Peugeot; such was Mike's access to resources. I had clearly moved on to this new life and despite the desire I saw burning within my mother to make me stay, make me finish the path she'd wanted for me, there was nothing to be done.

I left home and kept my tears to myself until Mike closed the door of the car. It was not his fault any more than it was my mother's so I kept the sobs as quiet as possible as we made our way down the long road to Nairobi and to our new home. By the time I could see the city through the windshield of *our* car, I had exhausted myself with crying and had been swallowed by that numbness that comes after a long, hard cry.

"It is only a short delay, Njoki. I will see to it that you return to school and get your degrees. It is more than just something your mother wants. You want this as well and I'll not take it from you."

Fresh tears poured from my eyes and I reached across the car to hold his hand for the rest of the drive.

The last time I had cried like this was when I learned that my brother Anthony had been killed in a car accident, leaving behind his wife and young children. I still remember the devastation I felt on hearing the news and then the sensation of falling before everything went dark.

Later, the nuns told me that I had fainted. They sent me home, saying that I would not have to return to school. I remembered hearing that and insisting that I be allowed to return after some time off and continue my education. At the time, the decision was a difficult one but I am glad for it now. No matter what the state of my life, I've always known that my education was a priority and I'm glad to have put it first so often. And, I was even more grateful that my education was important to my husband as well.

As we pulled into a parking spot on the street, I could hear the shouts of the merchants, the roar of the car engines and was nearly overwhelmed. Mike walked me to his house, our home now, and opened the ornate door at the top of the short staircase. The building wasn't as big as the church, but I still got the feeling I was walking into a sacred place.

If I was unsure that my life was changing before that moment, I became certain as the door opened to reveal the sweet smell of food cooking in an oven and flowers on the dining table, though I could see neither just yet. The entryway had a plush red carpet leading down the hall and I marvelled at the richness of the colour and the soft cushion beneath my feet.

I had truly never seen anything like this before. There were carpets and framed pictures and electricity. There were gold candelabras, chandeliers in the dining room – an actual, separate dining room – and a fireplace with a mantle. Something occurred to me only then. I had married this man; these things were now our things.

Did that mean I had lots of money?

Did it mean I was a princess and I was going to live in a castle and be happy forever after?

Was this the play that I had participated in while in primary school where my role was a princess who was rescued by a prince who became human when I hit him with a lemon because before that he was a green frog?

All kinds of memories were racing through my head. This was not real.

The little girl in me recalled the double-decker beds in the dormitories of my primary school and I wondered if our children would be given one of those coveted spots with the mattresses instead of slipping wood planks.

How important were we now?

Would our children warrant such luxuries?

After a dinner the likes of which I had never tasted, we went to bed and once again I was struck by the sheer opulence of the room. One might think I would favour the four-poster bed, the ensuite bathroom or the rich curtains.

But really, the feature that struck me as the most luxurious, the most representative of my new station in life was the white sheets. They were not the grey of unbleached cotton or slightly pink from too many washings without enough soap.

They were pure, bright white and I told myself, Yes, Njoki. You have arrived – your husband has a car, a carpeted house, long drapes that touch the floor, house help, different dinner sets, crystal glasses, wine glasses – and oh my God – I am sure lots of money in his account. Yes, Njoki, you are wealthy. Look at all this! Your sheets are white and you have a real mattress. This is what rich people have.

World Views

I'm up in the air, crossing the continent of Africa on my way to South Africa. I've been invited to present my paper on Indigenous healing. How strange that I travel back to Africa, to teach about *Africa*. I suppose that countries grow and mature, just like people do and we all tend to forget the little details of our past. It's only through our shared memories that we ever truly know where we came from. It seems that no one person, book or photograph can preserve every detail.

Is it only coincidence that my ideas for this "world views" chapter come to me as I soar over the African soil? I don't think so. Inspiration comes full circle and on this journey back home, I find clarity about the journey that led me from it. The pilot calls our attention to the desert below and I lean over to peek out the oblong window. Before my eyes, peeking out between bundles of clouds, is the Sahara. I still marvel at the speed of travel. These planes cover a distance in seconds more than what my mother's feet could cover in days of walking with me on her back.

And now, here I am on Mother Africa's back, right where it all began; at the core, the source. It is this core that I have struggled to reconnect with. It has seemed so distant, so diluted that only returning to the well could fill me again. I've spent most of my life preparing to leave Africa, and it seems that now I will spend the rest of my life trying to find her again.

My family sent me away to the missionaries to get an education and educated I became. But I have always worried that something was missing, that some vital piece had been left out of this vast accumulation of knowledge. As if it was all information with no wisdom to be found. This paper I am presenting is one attempt of many to reconnect with that African wisdom, about my Indigenous ways. These are the ways my parents taught me long before the missionaries organized my mind into one of a student of books. I was once a student of Africa and now I am again.

My presentation is more than just the knowledge that has been preserved by many people in many books. It is about what is missing from these books and papers. It is about the core of Africa; fragmented but not yet completely destroyed. I reach out and touch this core, in the depths of my soul, when times are tough. I hold the folder containing my paper tightly; it's far too early in my trip for its presence to be about preparation.

Right now, this paper is so much more than gathered knowledge, cue cards for a speech or even a record of things past. It is the thread that extends back through time, which sews me to the African soil and refuses to let go. Without such threads in all of us, our origins would slip away like so much water through our fingers, wasted and forgotten.

"Mama," I pray, "let us pull the threads together, help me to weave them into an airtight, waterproof mat. Let me be wrapped in it so no more of this ancient energy will be lost in the void of forgetfulness. I cannot afford to waste any more of this precious energy."

Looking around the plane at the many different people occupying these seats, I marvel at how much my life has changed, how my perspective has shifted. It all plays out before me, just behind my eyes, like a movie projected without a screen to contain it.

My early life, pure and innocent, still clinging to the memories of my mother's morning rituals, calling out to our Creator to bless our day, thanking our Creator for giving her family another day. This ritual centred me, gave me focus; this was my centre and as I left my bed and stepped out to the rising sun, I knew I was not alone.

The Ena River – it was everything imaginable. The river was the source of life, the space for recreation, a gathering point, a space where people, especially women, shared stories, counselled each other and provided emotional support. Ena River was my world – up to this day, the river has never left me. Whenever I dream about it, I know it is a reminder, I am walking too far from my centre – from my world view.

Our village. Everyone knew everyone else. Parents were parents for all children. Other people's concerns were everyone's concerns. The world revolved around news from the chief. There was communal oneness, cohesion, collective responsibility, everything was relational; the land, its produce, became a common-cohesive-grounded rural world view.

Ena Primary School, across the river, was the first marker of moving away from my rural world view. I remember little of my four years in that school, but they were happy years. And at the end of the four years, I was crowned a princess before I went home, where my mother's evening ritual reconnected me, reminded me of who I was and the importance of giving thanks.

Sacred Heart Girls School, a boarding school for girls, was where the rural world view was shattered and regiment was introduced. Notions of good and evil were injected into my world view, routinized and crystallized with prayers interspersed throughout the day. The solemnization of this regiment was interspersed with Irish dancing and occasional freestyle dancing. My first disconnect, moving away from my rural world view as foreign, mission-centric ideologies became my new world view and pushed my rural views to the subconscious. This mission-centric world view later enabled me to fly like a bird and soar in the clouds as I crossed different oceans, continents and deserts.

I decided I needed to pray and work really hard for either my sister to rescue me or my education. My prayers were answered, and from grade eleven on my sister would pick me up during the holidays and take me to the city.

What a joy to play with her children; I spent my time longing for a Western lifestyle, to live in a big house. My visit to my sister's home created a longing and reassurance that my parents had done the right thing to send me to a missionary boarding school.

My sister, the first woman whom I saw riding a bicycle, then a motorbike, was truly Westernized. I wanted to be like her and wear red lipstick and polish my finger- and toenails red. I was on my way to a Western lifestyle, like my older sister, whose little girls were always dressed like butterflies. Once I had been taught within the mission-centric view, the drill was simple; all you need is prayer and hard work and the city life will be part of you. Yes, city life that my older sister enjoyed became engrained in me.

But then all this dream life was ruptured when I travelled to North America for more education, which, along with my travels to Europe, created doubts. What would hold my life together? The village? The rivers? The city? The home country? My relatives? My children or friends?

I have travelled many miles over the years, and have been introduced to many schools of thought through formal and informal learning. Each setting made a lasting impression and subtly shifted who I was going to become. When I was exposed to Eurocentric paradigms for the first time, I *loved* it! So fascinating, yet so far away and so foreign. I tried to run toward it, to embrace it and make it part of my own core but it kept eluding me, even when I travelled in search of it. I have also experienced the world of insincerity, half-truths and injustice, and a world in which most are concerned only with "what's in it for me?" A world of exploitation, unhealthy competition, unhealthy foods and drinks.

And all the while, the inner me was screaming to be released, to be unchained, to revisit the teaching of my parents; the *rural* world view. Where everything was held together by core principles, relationality, mutual respect for people, land, environment, mutual stretching, collective and communal responsibility where we had ancestral grounding, affirmed by ceremonies and rituals. But how can I go back to that world view? How can that be possible when I am twenty-two thousand kilometres from Ena River, my parents' graveyard, the familiar sounds of birds, crickets, frogs … the familiar sounds and rhythms of Africa?

How can that be possible when Kirinyaga – the mount with an ostrich head, the mountain where our Creator resides – is not visible at all? The inner voice keeps telling me it's possible – it *is* possible. The sounds of crickets, drums, waves from Ena River, the women's laughter as they share their stories by the riverside while they wait for their clothes to dry, are still *intact*.

They are in my soul; the ancestral teachings are engraved in my heart.

All the morning rituals still echo with the first rays of the sun. Yes! The core is intact – I just have to reach out into my subconscious, hold it tight and breathe it in again. Make it my own and let it guide me in everything I do. The African rhythms live in me. I do not have to travel far to experience them – unless I decide to mask them the way

I have done for decades, until now. And I have suffered for it.

Let the African sunrise glow on the horizon as a new epoch begins. I make a commitment to myself, to live a life of peace, a life that is reflective and meditative, a life of gratitude and thankfulness for small and big mercies, a life that I can look into other people's eyes and let them know I do care. I *do* care for their well-being in my own way, in ways they might not understand at the moment, but ways that would be revealed to them.

That will be the new me ... the renewed me, the *energized* me. I had drifted away. The new Njoki will operate from a place of sincerity, serenity, honesty and love. I know the world will give me back what I give to it. My world will be guided by positive energy, surrounded by my guiding pillars: connectivity, sincerity, collectivity, responsibility, reciprocity, honesty and mutuality.

This renewed energy had different names – African world view, Afrocentric world view, Africanity – and they are all mine.

Conversations with Anthony

My new high school for girls is far from Ena; it is really far because my mother cannot even take me there. We cannot walk to the school; she cannot carry my suitcase on her head. My sister and her husband come to pick me up in her car. I feel special. Both will take me to the new school, but first, I will spend a night in Nairobi. What a treat.

I have been at my new school for two months. Then I have this weird dream. In my dream, I see someone walking down a path, walking away from me and suddenly disappearing.

What am I supposed to make of this?

The following morning, we all gather on the bus and make our way to Nairobi. We're on our way to watch a play. My friends and I all chat on the way there about what we're going to see, whether or not the play will be of any interest and what we'll do with our few hours of free time. Though I'm actively involved in our conversation, I can't seem to shake the feeling that something is wrong.

The journey to Nairobi is without incident and as we off-load from the bus, I am once again overcome with delight at the sights of this modern city. The playhouse is just down the street and we all line up, eager to make our way to the building where our entertainment for the day awaits.

On our way back from the playhouse, I see someone jogging behind us; a young man who looks vaguely familiar, even from this distance. As he approaches, my chest tightens again with the same unease that my dream brought to me.

The young man slows down as he nears our group and I realize that he must have some news for someone in our school. He approaches one of the nuns and whispers something in her ear. The expression on the nun's face does not change and, for a moment, I think that perhaps the news is not bad news. But when both of their faces turn, eyes finding me, I hold my breath as ice races through my veins.

I recognize this young man.

He is from my village and the news that he has raced to bring to our group is clearly for me. As the two of them approach, my friends tug at my arm, trying to gain my attention.

"Catherine," they whisper. "What is this about? Who is that man?"

I can't seem to muster the focus to answer. My mind ricochets back and forth between my dream and the approaching pair.

"Catherine," the nun states, voice even and firm. "This young man has brought news from your village."

The nun turns to him, urging him to speak.

"Njoki," he starts, reverence and sadness imbuing his voice. "Njoki, I am so sorry. I am so sorry."

"Who?" I ask, frozen with the knowledge that this news will change my life, forever.

He stutters for a moment, the weight of his task clearly taxing his will to deliver his message.

"Njoki, it's Anthony. He died in a car accident. I'm so sorry. Today was his burial – June 14 ...."

No.

No, not Anthony.

Not Anthony with a wife and his lovely children. What will happen to his wife and children? Not Anthony, my handsome, tall brother. Strong, wise, wonderful Anthony who always buys me Nivea cream to make sure my skin is smooth and beautiful, who attended the Kikuyu Teachers College so he could help my parents afford to send the rest of us to school. Anthony who has a twin, Henry, a twin who will be absolutely crushed by this news.

It cannot be.

He cannot be the one from my dream.

It's not fair.

As the reality of it all hits me, I feel my world tilt and everything fades.

I don't remember hitting the ground. The nuns say that I fainted and I suppose it should worry me, but I feel nothing beyond this all-consuming numbness. I barely remember the drive back to the school and by the time we return, my sister and her husband have come to pick me up. The nuns called them as soon as I fainted. They have come to take me to kijiji – to visit my brother's graveyard and to be with family at this time of mourning.

"She has been overcome," one of the nuns tells my sister. "She will be excused from school."

"No," I whisper. "No, I will return. Give me time and I will return."

They both observe me for a moment, seeming to absorb what I've said, but I pay little attention to them and whether or not they believe me. The drive home is long, over two hours because of the fog and I feel nothing but the cold emptiness of Anthony's death.

I take nearly three months off school to mourn and recover from the shock and devastation Anthony's death has brought to our family. The next two years of school are so much more difficult. Focus is a strain on my lean resources, but I know the last thing Anthony would want is for me to stop learning and abandon my path.

Sometimes I dream of him, other times I have conversations with him. I can feel his spirit with me and cherish the guidance he offers during our long conversations. More than once he has walked me through hopeless situations and I long to repay him for all that he has given to me, even after his passing.

So, when the time comes to aid his family, I jump at the opportunity. In my own little way, I made a promise to Anthony to make sure that I will assist his family as much as I can, and in particular I will take responsibility for Wanjuki's education. It is therefore without hesitation that I find Wanjuki a high school where she can complete form five and six, the equivalent of grade eleven and twelve in Canada. At this time I am married, but a student at Kenyatta University. I reach out to Anthony while I am at school and he guides me in this effort.

"Go to university, Sister; share your worries with your friend Ruth. You'll find what you're looking for."

Nairobi is, of course, where the university is and nearly an hour's drive from where I am currently obtaining a first degree. Nevertheless, the message is clear and as soon as I arrive at the college, I go searching for Ruth. I find her in the library and share with her my dilemma. However, as I complete sharing my story, I mention to her that I have an answer to what I am looking for and if she wouldn't mind accompanying me to a high school that is about ten kilometres from the university.

Once there, I ask the principal whether they have vacancies in their form five and his answer is no. It is at that moment that Ruth says to me, "Catherine, I have an idea. If you are willing to drive your Mercedes for three hundred kilometres, we can take your niece to my sister's school." I jump in the car and tell my friend I am not afraid to drive. However, we can take a driver with us. For the next few hours, I concentrate on what is required for Wanjuki and before five in the afternoon we arrive at Ruth's sister's school, which is located in the Rift Valley. Just as we reach the administrative office, I recognize someone. She waves at me and we make our way to the office.

"Hello, Njoki! What brings you here?"

"Hello! I'm so glad to see you. We're actually here to find out if we can help someone. What do you do here?"

"I'm head of admissions for this school, but Ruth's sister is the headmistress."

Thank you, Anthony!

I produce Wanjuki's examination papers. She had passed very well and the admission's officer did not hesitate to admit her. In the meantime, Ruth had left us and had gone to chat with her sister, who joins us later with some news.

"Ruth tells me you're looking for a spot for your niece. You are very lucky. You see, we've just had a cancellation from someone we invited last year. I happen to have a place to fill and I would be happy to have your niece join our school." We leave for Nairobi that night, thrilled to know that little Wanjuki will be going to school in the morning and that I was able to do something for Anthony and his daughter.

A few weeks later, I hear from Anthony again. His gratitude is clear and so is the impression that he has done what he needed to do and will no longer be *answering* my calls.

"Let me rest now, Njoki. My task is done and you are no longer in need of my guidance."

"Thank you, Anthony. I will miss you."

Promises and Burials

Father died when he was over 120 years old. He'd made it clear to all of us that he wanted to be buried in a concrete plot so that his body would be preserved and never touch the dirt. I'd thought for many years that it was such an odd request, especially since our custom was to bury people in the dirt and allow their bodies to return to the land.

Of course, I never got the chance to ask him why he wanted such a thing. It seemed so odd that he would want to be buried in such a cold place, disconnected from the land and forever separated from our ancestors who were buried in the dirt long ago. Sometimes I wondered if the answers to many of my questions about my father are hidden in that mysterious journal of his. I still remember the way he used to write in it every morning.

After his death, my father's belongings were divided up amongst all the sons from both my father's wives. The journal went to one of my older brothers, and to my knowledge, he has not shared the journal with his siblings. For my last visit with Dad, I came from Canada and brought Sein to see her grandfather. As soon as we approached the compound, he told us he knew we were coming and, reaching into his pocket, he gave me a bill of twenty shillings and gave Sein his drinking horn that was especially designed for him.

Dad always drank his honey beer from this horn or from a bottle; it was, therefore, special to have this rare gift given to one of my daughters. But my interest was in the journals. It would seem that the contents of my father's journals may forever remain a mystery. Mugeni, my brother, has promised to search for them; however, he has not managed to get them – and I will not have a page of this diary in my book!

I often wonder what he would have thought or how he would have reacted the day I graduated with my Ph.D. He and my mother gave up so much to ensure that I would have an education and be free of our village rather than being married young. By the time I returned to school after giving birth to my second child with Mike, both my parents had given up on me. Mike reassured them that he would do what it took for me to obtain a university education. His singular focus during that time was to keep his promise to my mother and make sure I finished my college degree.

On the day I found out I had passed and that I was on the honours list, I was overwhelmed with emotion and I could not wait to drive to the kijiji to let them know of my accomplishment. I remember calling Mike to share the news and his response was, "Why don't you treat yourself to a hairdo and a massage, or lunch in one of your favourite restaurants and then meet me at home?" I could not make out his coldness; I thought, What is his problem?

I had a university degree and that was what mattered, but I drove to my salon, had a hair wash and massage and I drove home. My only thought was to create some time in the course of the week to see my parents and share the good news. I practised in my mind everything I would say, repeat to my mother every promise I'd made and reassure her that I would keep each of those promises by graduating.

When I arrived at my home, there were cars parked everywhere and people standing outside. I recognized many of them as friends and family and I smiled and waved as I headed to the front door. I doubted they'd seen me because I was moving so quickly and I thought nothing of the fact that they didn't wave or smile in return.

I went straight to the kitchen to ensure that the cook had everything under control because I was sure Mike called our friends so that we could celebrate my graduating from university. I saw one of my brothers who immediately wrapped his arms around me. I couldn't help but smile and laugh at the quickness of his greeting. And then he spoke: "I'm so sorry, Njoki."

Sorry?

What was he sorry for?

What a mean thing to say on the day I found out about my results!

"What are you talking about? Why are you sorry?"

I pulled away from his embrace and finally looked at his face. His eyes were grave and the regret showed through.

"What is going on?" I asked, now terribly confused by his reaction.

"I'm sorry," he whispered, pulling away completely and walking into the next room.

I turned to my cousin Wanjuki, who had come in shortly after I did.

"Njoki," she started with that same grave tone. "This morning, Aunt passed way. I am so sorry."

"What do you mean by this? What do you mean! My mother is not gone. I obtained my results today. My graduation is in two weeks and both my parents have to be there. They have to witness their daughter graduating."

My voice rose to a near-shouting volume. Adrenaline coursed through my body and I could feel myself shaking. This could not be right. My mother was not dead. She was supposed to be here to see that I had kept my promise and obtained a degree. I had to show it to her. She had to touch it and feel it in her hands.

Mama, tell me that these people are playing with me.
Mama, no you cannot die now,
   not now when I have kept my promise.
Mama, I have so many stories to tell you about my
      journey,
   my journey to getting my degree.
Mama, did you forget I still had some reading to do for
      you?
Oh Mama, Mama, you can't have crossed.

Crossed to the other side without goodbye.
Mama, tell me I am dreaming,
dreaming about you and soon I will wake up.
Oh, I am falling, yes, Mama, I am falling –
But I don't fall, Mama.
I can see your arms ready to hold me.

Someone embraced me and I was too confused to respond. I heard words being spoken but had no presence of mind to listen to them. My thoughts raced to catch up with what I'd been told, but the pieces just wouldn't fit together. Eventually, I sat down at the table and allowed myself the time to process what I'd been told.

This was what I'd rushed home for. It couldn't be. I was disappointed when I did not receive flowers or some kind of acknowledgement when I drove to my compound. Now that disappointment seemed so foolish in the face of the reason behind the absence. I thought of my father and how he might have taken the news of his wife dying. Who would prepare meals for him? Who would wash his clothes? Could he move to live with us?

My father was much older than my mother. He was supposed to die before her; it wasn't supposed to be like this: older people die first. I guess in my parents' case, it was different. My young mother died before she celebrated her seventieth birthday, without a grey hair on her head. I suppose I assumed that my mother would live to be as old as Dad. And now she was gone. She had become invisible energy. I could not hold her, feel her. She was gone and I'd kept my promise, but it was too late.

In the days after my mother's death, I tended to the burial and ensured that her wishes were honoured. Unlike my father, Mother wanted to be buried in the dirt with a tree planted over her grave. She once told me that the tree would draw strength from her body and grow to provide joy and shelter to the children that would someday play there. We purchased the small sapling, and we planted it. I made a promise to visit her grave as often as I could.

I have kept that promise, visiting every few years. The tree has grown large and I often sit under its shade and remember the times when I would lounge with my mother during her break from tending the fields, telling her stories and reading to her from my school books. Each time I visit her grave and sit under her tree, I read her a book or tell her a story of my own, revelling in the connection I feel with that tiny plot of land and all the memories and emotions it evokes.

During the thirtieth commemoration of Mama's transition, I thought I would do something special for her and my dad. I talked to all my siblings and we decided to cement her yard and renovate our dad's resting place. These days, when I visit Mum, I sit on the stone and continue our conversations. Sometimes I shed tears uncontrollably; other times, I am calm and I am attentive to what she has to say. A number of times, I have taken my children – her grandchildren – to the graveside and it has been refreshing to see them communicate with their grandparents who are in the spirit world. Sometimes neighbours stare at us as we sit on our parents' tombstone. But I am beyond embarrassment or explanation. My parents are beings who are in energy form and though I cannot see them, I can feel their presence.

I've kept my promises. I've earned multiple degrees, and have children and grandchildren. I remarried sometime after Mike died. My children are strong and smart and beautiful, just like their grandparents. They know where they came from and all that is available to them through their education, faith and family. I know Mama can see me now, and I'm sure she is proud of the woman I have become. I know that I am proud of her. My youngest daughter is named after my mother; she carries her spirit. Sometimes I worry that I put too much pressure on her; I want to be around her all the time. What she does not realize is that, through her, I see my mother. Seeing her gives me a great deal of comfort.

My two older children talk of my parents with lots of pride. They still remember our visits to see their grandparents. One of my sons carries both Mike's grandfather's family name and my dad's name. Sometimes I wonder whether that is too heavy for him, to carry the spirit of two ethnic groups whose cultures are very different from each other. My middle daughter bears the name of Mike's older sister, who mothered him after the death of his parents. My two youngest sons, Aziz and Moody, both bear the name Anthony, however for Aziz, Anthony is a middle name; while Moody is named after my late brother.

To You, Henry, My Brother

Henry, oh my brother, I am thinking of you.
Henry, you never told me you would be in the spirit
    world,
yes, Henry, the spirit world before my book was
    published.
Henry, the passing of your twin brother, Anthony,
our brother Anthony was devastating.
I still remember how much you suffered.
I still remember the period when you missed him so
    much.
Henry, I still remember,
remember the last time I visited you in hospital.
Henry, my brother, I miss you,
I wish I knew that this visit to hospital

would be the last time,

the last time to set my eyes on you.

Oh Henry, why didn't you tell me,

tell me the last time we talked about how you were
    feeling?

Henry, did you know in a couple of weeks –

Yes, Henry, weeks, you would be with your brother,

my brother, Henry, your twin brother, Anthony?

Henry, your last decade in your human body,

your last few years, earthly years were difficult.

Your body fought hard during that time,

yes, that time you thought you were exiting.

Exiting the earthly world,

Henry, you would joke about it.

Do you remember, how you would say;

I almost left –

Henry, I have so many questions to ask you.

Questions about this or that.

Questions about Mum and Dad.

Questions about life in general.

However, for now,

yes, for now, Henry, I will reserve those questions.

Those questions that I have no answers to,

until we meet again.

Asante, Henry, asante for all. Asante.

I wanted to say more, but tears,

tears, Henry, blur my eyes, I have to stop here.

Stop writing – before I sob out loud.

Oh Henry, I have to let you know.

I gathered courage and visited,

visited the hospital where you had your last breath

I cried, Henry.

I truly did, but I had to visit the place,

your last place in a human body.

Henry, it was hard – as I thought of you and Venancio.

Venancio, your brother-in-law who followed you.

Yes, three weeks only, and he joined you in the spirit
world.

Spirit world.

The Woman of the Two Worlds

I was born in Kenya, a country enriched by more than a thousand years of cultural exchange of Nilotic, Bantu, Hamitic and Cushitic language groups, whose lives were shaped by the fertility of the land, or lack of it. Kenya is a country of contrast and diversity. One cannot drive for three hundred kilometres without experiencing different landscapes, climate and terrain. Its northern and eastern regions occupy a high plateau where rainfall is sparse and the land is dry. Further south, the land sprouts shrubs and grasslands. In the southwestern highlands, part of the Great Rift Valley – a chain of lakes, valleys and volcanoes, including Mount Kilimanjaro – carves a magnificent swath that ultimately runs across much of Eastern Africa. And it is in Kenya, amid escarpments and scattered lakes, that one finds evidence of our earliest ancestors.

The wisdom acquired over many centuries from countless generations of varied peoples who lived and continue to live on this land reflects a deep respect for the environment that, along with the cultural crossover between major ethnic groups, formed the foundations of an Indigenous knowledge that has continuously evolved. These knowledges encompassed not only agricultural practices and methods, but also social and spiritual well-being. Formed by observation of the natural world, and dictated by the vagaries of the landscape, these peoples nurtured a healthy respect for the land and all living creatures on it, growing food crops for domestic sustenance and, often, trade. Maintaining this ability was integral to traditional practices, passed down from generation to generation through the centuries in the understandings of women who today engage in agricultural practices much as their forebears did. Their domestic food processing techniques are part of a wider Indigenous knowledge base that regrettably is under threat, first precipitated by colonization, and now by the onrush of globalization and modernity. Political, economic and social mores have changed and are still changing, but there are aspects of Kenyan Indigenous knowledge, as well as those of other African countries, that continue to motivate and sustain diverse ethnic cultures.

In August 1987 I arrived in Canada to pursue graduate studies at the University of New Brunswick in Fredericton. My curiosity to create new relationships and eagerness to learn made me question – question the absence of racialized and Indigenous Peoples in most of the classes or even any of the scholarship written by non-Caucasian people. I was pushed to engage in different kinds of research that placed Indigenous and Black Canadian people at the centre. In particular, due to scarcity of written scholarship on Africa and Kenya in particular, I decided to revisit the Indigenous teaching that I was exposed to while growing up in Kenya with the hope of theorizing land, taking on the responsibility of creating new knowledges and making sense of reconciliatory processes pertaining to the atrocities committed to the land and people. Most interesting is that all this is happening here in Canada, far from Africa. My research opened my eyes to the impact of colonialism, imperialism, colonial and neo-colonial education, the fragmentation of the self through religion and the dislocation of my being.

Kenya was under direct British rule for seventy-five years. Under British rule, the social structures were disrupted and damaged and people's cultural beliefs were devalued. The colonial government managed to create doubt in people's mind about who they were, to the point where parents advocated a colonial education for their children even after independence was attained in 1963. For instance, I attended missionary schools from grade five to grade twelve. All my teachers were white nuns, and I followed a British curriculum and memorized material written by Western scholars to pass British set examinations. I took pride in reading and reciting works of Shakespeare, D.H. Lawrence, George Bernard Shaw, Hemingway and Dickens, and I regarded others who did not read or enjoy reading these books as backwards and illiterate.

The education that I received reinforced strong Western values and created a desire to aspire to "whiteness." It should be understood that colonialization through education was actually part of a much bigger and lengthier process. All the teaching was embedded in a social structure designed to erode traditional knowledges and values. Colonial education succeeded in planting seeds for the expansion, growth and sustainability of imperialism. This is eloquently captured by Edward Said (*Orientalism*, 1978) as the "process or policy of establishing and maintaining an empire, lingering where it has always been in general cultural sphere as well as in specific political, ideological economic and social practices" (p. 9). In other words, education was an organized form of imperialism that allowed colonization to reproduce itself.

Unknown to me, the act of being schooled in the literary canons so valued in Europe caused me to be disassociated from and devalued the cultural knowledges and wisdom of my ancestors, my community and my family.

Visiting my homeland today, I cannot escape the constant lament of the elders about the destruction of the land, the deforestation, the dry riverbeds, the disrespect of the land. The elders blame the current generation for having no respect for the land. This is the land where I grew up. This is the place that was green, with rivers that used to house crocodiles, rivers that used to swallow women and children when either bathing or fetching water. When I hold conversations with youth about all the destruction, they dismiss me and say I have lost touch with reality. The current youth do not see the elders' defence of "traditional"/customary ways of taking care of the land and respecting the land. I tell the youth, respecting the land and keeping our African traditions does not imply local peoples want to live in the past nor are they only interested in glorifying or romanticizing the past for its own sake.

Rather, it is an astute realization that knowledge is cumulative. Knowledge builds on itself and only the anti-intellectual will claim some forms of knowledge as useless knowing, without appreciating the contexts and politics of claiming and producing such knowledge. Personally, I see that having a connection to the land, having a meaningful relationship with the land, will restore our sensibility. Growing up in rural Kenya, the land was everything to my family. I still remember the many stories that my parents would narrate to us as children on the importance of land. For instance, Mother would always remind us that when we take something from the land, we should give something back.

During harvest time, there were harvesting songs that my mother taught us. She told us that these songs were sung as women and men would scatter seeds from the previous years as a way of telling our Creator, we are here to harvest what you have provided for us, please accept our gifts of the seeds. I have found the grounds that my parents provided me with have enabled me to work with Indigenous knowledge as a strategic knowledge base from which to rupture the Western way of knowing and to create relationships with the people of Turtle Island. I am convinced that the knowledge I acquired growing up offers the best hope to create meaningful and sacred relationships with the people of Turtle Island. Having land as a discourse, as a common ground to begin our discussions, provides the bases of mutual learning and from which we can mount teachings from the land. Although the insistence upon the reimagining and repositioning of difference as critical political discourse draws strength from the important work of critical theorizing, I nevertheless further want to insist upon an Indigenous knowledge theoretical framework that enunciates itself in the talk of land, responsibility and reconciliation.

Reflection: Being Black, a Woman and a Professor in Canada

In April 2017, I travelled to Kenya for a fellowship program in a university not far from where I grew up. My mandate was to work with faculty and graduate students to develop two programs: a master's degree on Early Childhood Education and a second one on Leadership, Governance and Development Studies. I felt a sense of pride as I brainstormed with different members of this university to come up with two programs that spoke to them and that were African centred. Occasionally, I got lost in my thoughts when I remembered how my father would tell us about a school of agriculture and veterinary medicine that he co-founded in the early forties to teach farmers how to care for their farms and their cattle. Little did I know that, one day, I would be working in the institution at which he once taught in the forties. Yes, I am walking on the same soil that he did as a young man, who was very ambitious in transforming his own farming communities.

He taught many about grafting an orange with a lemon to produce a grapefruit. He taught farmers how to plant maize on a straight line instead of scattering the seeds. Of course, there was a lot of opposition from his own community members who had learnt traditional methods from their parents and grandparents. In addition, he introduced to his community artificial insemination. I'm not sure where he had learnt all this from, but somehow, his travels had exposed him to different farming methods.

I am not a scientist, nor do I enjoy farming, but I feel proud of my late dad. His impact is evident today, though he has gone unrecognized by his own community. Let me go back to my teaching, and why being back in Kenya as a visiting professor was very significant. I will never forget how one morning in May 2017, while I was in Embu town, I received an email with the subject line: President's Teaching Award. I thought, why should I open this email when it will give me bad news. I decided not to open it. After two days, I got another email, which said: Congratulations on your award. "What award?" I responded. "The President's Teaching Award," they replied.

I did not respond immediately. I broke down and cried. I cried tears of joy. I had received an award for something that I love doing – being a teacher – yes, a professor. Yet for days, I did not share the news with anyone. I was reflecting on what it meant to receive such an award despite all my challenges of being Black, female and teaching at a Canadian University.

As was my practice, I turned to my parents. I was grateful for their presence during my almost twenty years of being a professor at the University of Toronto. I was grateful for their encouragement, especially during those days when I felt I had had enough of teaching students who constantly questioned whether I was qualified enough to teach them; whether I had the theoretical foundation required to teach in one of the most prestigious universities in the world. I tell you, being Black, female and a professor in a predominantly European university could take a toll on you.

However, I did not allow that to happen to me. I had my parents, my invisible guardians who stood by me every step of the way. I think what challenged most of my students was this notion of having to dwell on anti-Black racism, Black feminist thought and critical race theories; to address issues of positive racial identity development for Black and other marginalized students in Ontario schools. I was at loggerheads with many of my students because I argued for the importance of challenging anti-Black racism in schooling while creating supportive spaces for expressions of healing and mutual understanding. I also emphasized the importance of knowing one's own history.

As I reflect on this award I tell myself that being a professor for almost twenty years and being part of the administration has been rewarding. I enjoy what I do. I enjoy teaching. I take challenging moments as learning moments for me or as teachable moments for others. I shed a tear as I think of Mum, Dad, my late brothers and Mike, the father of my children. I know all of them would have been proud of my accomplishments as an educator and educational leader and as a professor who has received many awards, not just this last one. With an aching heart, I hold myself tight. Why does life have to be so unfair? Why did you all leave for the spiritual world so prematurely?

I start thinking of what Anthony would have said to me or what my mom would have said, though to tell you the truth, I am not sure what they would have said. I know my mum would have chuckled and not uttered a word. My dad would have reminded me that I need to do more for the community – I need to be a doctor for all members of the community. It is interesting that at this particular time, I thought first of my relatives in the spirit world. What about the living relatives? Did I think of them then? I did, but after my initial emotions. After I had spent time with my spiritual guides, I could commune with my earthly relatives. And I did.

Why was it important to receive the news of my award in Kenya? As an award-winning teacher – I've been nominated for TVO Best Lecturer, received the African Women Achievement Award, the Harry Jerome Professional Excellence Award and the prestigious David E. Hunt Award for Excellence in Graduate Education – receiving the news of the President's Teaching Award for my contributions to teaching, learning and student supervision at the graduate level was a way of connecting everything I had learnt.

The journey of being a professor started here in Kenya, as a dream, when I was eight years old. The fulfillment of that dream was not a straight line from point A to point B.

It was a journey full of twists and turns. But I still got there. I still made it to the top of my profession, not at my original birthplace, but far, far away from my village – in Toronto, a city that glittered with thousands of lights as compared to my village, which was illuminated every thirty days by moonlight. There were no street lights, just the sun during the day and the stars and the moon at night. As you read this, I want you to imagine the endless possibilities that lie ahead of each one of us. As my parents used to say during the many occasions of their teachings: "No matter how long the night, dawn would come." My dawn was here and I was going to swallow its glory and imagine myself on top of Mount Kenya, shouting to the world, "I am a very good professor." Believe me. Sit and relax and let me finish my tale. If you are in Kenya, get hold of a nice cup of tea, switch off your radio or whatever you enjoy watching or listening to, and if you are in Toronto, put down your phone or your tablet, relax and come with me as I trace back my steps one last time – like the Sankofa Bird.

Journeying Back to My First Boarding School

I have been in Kenya for exactly three months and one day. It is August 8, 2018. Since my arrival, I have been dreading what I am going to do today. I plan to visit Sacred Heart Girls School, my first boarding school, and the hospital beside the school where my dad, Henry and Venacio passed on. I have been driving past these places for three months now. Crossing the Ngirimari, the river that the nuns used to take us to every single Saturday to wash our clothes. Just visualize that, small girls, all under fifteen, carrying turai, round tin basins, on their heads in a single line, with a head teacher at the front and a sister at the rear. Every time I drive over the river, emotions are evoked by sad memories. Memories of denial, of a sense of dislocation and a lack of grounding. This despite the fact that the place has changed so much, the river is no longer a big stream lined with stones where we used to spread our clothes to dry, but a tiny little stream that is hardly visible from the main road. The tiny bridge that we used to cross has been replaced by a broad road over an earthen bridge. If I did not know this place from the past, I would not have known that there is river underneath the massive amount of soil. I see the image of my mother, and tears roll down my cheeks. I still remember her standing on the opposite side of the road as she watched the line of little girls walk past her, trying to see if she could spot her daughter. I still remember seeing Mum and recoiling, trying to hide my face.

Mum – why did you have to come today, of all days?
Now everyone will see you.
My mother, wearing no shoes.
Mother, do you know how strict this nun is?
Will you have the courage to walk to her because I will not?
Oh Mother, Mother – why are you doing this to me?
Mum, forgive me my naïveté.
Forgive my foolishness.
Forgive my ignorance.
Mum, who cares today whether you are wearing shoes or
     not?
I wish I could be given a chance to be a child again.
To walk down this path and see you and let the world know –
know that you are my mother.
The woman of my heart,
the woman who never let me down.
The woman who would walk for miles –

miles and miles without shoes to see her child.
Mama, walk with me today. Come with me.
I will be visiting my school, and
the hospital where your husband,
my dad, and
your son, and
your son-in-law passed on.
Hold me, Mum.
My body is weak.
My emotions are raw.
I have been crying in anticipation,
anticipation of the school, the church, the hospital.

As I turn onto the road to the school, I am actually sobbing so loudly I fear I will faint. I recall the number of times
I walked on this road barefoot. I drive up to the gate of the
school and stop. There was no gate during my school days.
A lady comes with a book to register my entry – she sees me
crying and she asks me whether there is something wrong.

"No. I have come to visit my old school."

"Okeyyy – why are you crying then?"

I am crying because all of a sudden, all my emotions
cannot be contained, the church and baby Jesus, the nuns,
the wooden beds – I take the book, and tears are falling
on the open page. "I am sorry for crying . . . I am just overwhelmed." The lady looks at me as if I have lost my mind.
I heard her say to herself, "There must be something else
that is making this woman cry – I do not believe it is just
the visit to the school." Inside me, I know she is right. It is
not just the school, it is the many losses that are identified

with this place. My brother, my dad and my brother-in-law had all died in a hospital not far from this school. This is the same school where I walked barefoot for three years. This is the same school where I decided to change my name. Yes, there is much more than just the visit.

By that time, I have written my name, given her back her book and driven through the gate and I find myself facing the church. I stop abruptly. What happened to our cathedral? I look at the rear window and I see the lady from the gate walking toward my car. I wait for her.

"What happened to the cathedral – the big church?" I ask her. "Was the big church demolished?"

"Njoki," she says and I looked at her.

"How do you know my name?"

"You signed it in the book – and my name is also Njoki." The lady, a security guard, is visibly worried. First the crying, and now this abrupt stop of my car? I am sure she thinks there must be a problem here – as she approaches, I notice her eyes are full of concern and her voice indicates as much.

"Oh, oh, how are you, Njoki? It is always good to meet someone with the same name." I pause and go back to my first question. "So, Njoki, what happened to the big church?"

"The big church." She pauses. "What do you mean, the big church? This church was built by the missionaries in the late fifties. Nothing has changed." She looks at me for a moment. "Maybe it is you who has changed. From a little girl to a grown woman. When we are small, we see things differently. Everything is huge, big . . . It is still the same church. The only thing that might have changed is the people in charge of the church and the school. We have

African priests, African nuns and African teachers." She stops and points to the school compound. "Park your car there and see for yourself."

I park the car and enter the church. Many things have remained the same. They still have Jesus hanging on the cross – although this time, it is brown Jesus. They have Mary, mother of Jesus, holding baby Jesus – still in the same place as I remember, still a blue-eyed and blonde lady. Jesus's picture, where he is also blond and blue-eyed, showing his heart before he ascended to heaven, is next to his mother. I pay my respects before I take more pictures and walk down the aisle. As I walk, I ask myself, how many times have I walked down this path? How many have asked the questions that I ask today? For some strange reason, I am not emotional at all as I leave the church and head to the school.

I follow the same route that we used to follow after leaving the church. This time, there is a gate; I stop and sign again in another book and ask whether I can walk around the school. A young lady gives me permission and I enter. The same building that used to house grades five, six and seven still stands. Nothing has changed. I can see the nuns, hear their voices and their soft footsteps. I stop and start crying. I can still remember the occasion when the nun stopped the whole school and called me out for kneeling down facing the door instead of the alter. I pause for a moment reliving it and sob loudly. Was it necessary for her to slap me so hard?

However, in front of *my* building and behind it, there are other buildings: administration blocks. I ask the young lady to take me to see the dormitories. She asks me whether I am okay – whether I need to sit down. I tell her that I am fine – and then I start to laugh, laugh uncontrollably. I think to myself, so this is what it takes to create a prominent professor, but out loud I say, "What a journey." I wished the nuns, those who taught me about the Bible, or who slapped me when I was *wrong*, were here today. I would have given them big hugs and said, "Thank you. Thank you for making me toe the line."

We walk to the dormitories in silence. The corrugated wall has been demolished as well as the dormitories. Instead, there is a row of concrete buildings. I ask the young woman accompanying me about the long pipe that students used to use for washing in the morning, and she says that it no longer exists. However, as we walk in between the dormitories, I see something familiar looking. It is the thing – the pipe. I break down and start sobbing again. All of a sudden, I see a row of students standing facing each other and the pipe separating them. I hear the voice of the nun . . . and I wait for the water to flow. But there is no water. I am in a trance and I cannot move. When I snap out of it, I say to my guide, "There is no water?"

"No, this pipe is no longer operated; each dormitory has something similar to what you are describing at the rear end of each one of them."

"Oh."

I start walking back to the car without looking back. I say goodbye to the lady, thank her and leave. Somehow, I am at peace and I ask myself why I hadn't done this earlier.

From My Mother's Back

I loved being on my mother's back; from there, I could listen to her conversations with other women, I could observe her as she cooked and cleaned, as she bargained when she went shopping in Indian stores, but what I loved most was her cooking. It was always so sweet and warm. Someday, I'd tell myself, I will learn how to cook food like her, prepare a meal like her and everyone will love all the tasty things I would make. Mother used to laugh when I told her these things and that made me happy because she was usually so serious.

"Little Njoki," she would say. "You are so young, my daughter, barely four years. Why do you think so far ahead? Why not just play with your friends like the other girls do?"

"I do play. I play all the time and we pretend to be like you. We wash and cook things and take care of babies so when it is our turn, we'll be very good!"

"I'm sure you'll be very good, Njoki. Now, are you ready to go?"

That day we were going to the market for food and some cloth. This was my first time to the market and I was very excited. One of my best friends was Rafiki and her father had a shop in the market. I wondered if we'd see him.

"Njoki, are you ready?"

"Yes, Mama, I'm ready."

It was a long walk to the market and my feet started to hurt after only part of the way. The hot soil was burning the soles of my bare feet and I looked to my mother, hoping she'd notice and pick me up. At first she didn't and I huffed.

"What are you making all that noise for, Njoki?"

"My feet hurt, Mama. The road is hot and it's burning my feet."

She looked down at me, thinking for a moment before unwrapping a long cloth from her hips. Mother knelt down and I climbed up on her back, staying still while she wrapped the cloth around both of us to keep me from falling off. After she was sure that I was wrapped up tight, she started walking again and the gentle rhythm of her footsteps lulled me to sleep under the hot sun.

I stirred when I heard the noise of the market up ahead. Perking up immediately, I peered over her shoulder, desperate to see where all the sounds were coming from. We were still too far away for me to make out any of the details, but I strained anyway, craning my neck and squinting my eyes in an effort to improve my vision. It didn't work and I realized that only my mother's feet would get us close enough for me to see anything.

"Mama, what are we going to get?"

"Many things, Njoki. We're going to fill this basket with some cloth, thread and needles for clothes and some soaps to wash with. Will you help me find each of the shops we need?"

I was delighted to be involved in our shopping adventure.

"Yes!" I cry. "I'll help you find everything. Do I have to get down?"

"No, Njoki. You'll stay right there. Can you see?"

I checked to be sure, looking from one side to the other, manoeuvring around my mother's head and testing how far ahead I could see by twisting this way and that.

"I can see, Mama."

"Good. We're nearly there."

Mama was a tall woman, which meant I could see much further than some of the other children wrapped in a cloth and attached to their mother's back. As we got closer and closer to the market, I could see more people just like us going about their tasks for the day. Some were setting up their shops, arranging things on tables and pulling back curtains while others were shoppers like us, observing each item before moving to the next.

In the distance, I could hear some of them arguing over prices. I hoped we didn't have to do that because some of them were very loud and seemed to get angry.

We arrived at the market and walked slowly through the pathways, reviewing our options and checking the quality of the fruits and cloth. There were so many pretty things all around us, and not just the things for sale. There were many women in the market dressed in colourful and bright clothes, hair wrapped and piled on top of their heads. Many carried large baskets on their heads and normally my mother would too but she kept it on her hip today for my sake.

The reds and yellows and browns teased my eyes and I followed each woman as she walked by us until she was too far to see, fascinated with every detail. There were men in the market as well, some in robes like the men in my village and some in suits like my father. I wondered if they worked for the government with my father and was about to ask my mother before I thought better of it. I was supposed to be looking for clothes, not asking questions about my father.

"Do you see anything yet?" Mother asks.

See anything? Sure.

See what I'm supposed to be looking for?

Not yet.

"No, Mama, no seeds or cloth yet."

"Okay, let's keep looking."

I knew she knew exactly where we were supposed to go. She was taking me around the market, rather than straight to the stalls we needed because this was my first time here and she wanted to let me see. I love my mother so much. She always looked out for what was best for me and gave me so much every day. I hope someday I'm just like her and I hope my daughters love me as much as I love her.

As we moved closer, I realized that the stalls were on top of some odd-looking rock. I try to take a closer look, leaning out from my wrap and balancing myself on my mother's shoulder.

"Njoki, what are you doing? Stop that! You're going to fall."

Mother's hand quickly reached up and shoved me back into balance on her back.

"Sorry, Mama," I said, embarrassed at my mistake.

I knew better than to lean like that. We could both fall.

"What is that rock?"

"What are you talking about?" she replied, looking back to where I'd been pointing.

"That," I said, unhelpfully.

Still, like she always did, she knew exactly what I was talking about.

"That is concrete. It's like stone, but you can make it soft and then hard again with water. The market stalls are on top of concrete."

How strange!

Is this concrete only used in the market?

It must be very special rock. I bet the market was the only place I'd ever seen it. Doing my best to memorize every detail, I stared at the concrete floors of each stall, certain that I'd never see it again. Eventually, we truly began our search and Mother made her way to the first stall where seeds were sold to farmers.

Mother and the shopkeeper disagreed on price, but they didn't shout like the other people did. Mother stayed serious and finally got her way, paying the price they agreed upon and we moved on, leaving the grumbling shopkeeper behind us. Next was the cloth, which Mother let me help with choosing. I tried to pick pretty patterns and the two of us often agreed on which bits to buy.

We were done with our tasks far too soon and set back on the road to Ena. I looked forward to returning home and finishing our tasks for the day but every so often I peeked behind us, thinking about the market and all I had seen that day.

I wanted to see concrete and colourful clothes again. I wanted to see men in suits and foods being sold. I wanted to learn how to buy and sell and teach my own children how to do the same. But most of all, I wanted to be as tall as my mother when I grew up. The view from her back was so wonderful. I could see in every direction, there was nothing blocking my path and I could have anything I wanted so long as she was with me. My mother held me high and I could see that anything was possible.

AFTERWORD

To Doctor Professor Mama, From Us, Your Children

Childhood is a happy time. We view the world with innocent lenses untainted from the harsh reality of the challenges we will face as adults. Childhood is special because it equips us with tools that our parents struggle to provide, which help to chisel our future paths. This book has given us an opportunity to have a glimpse of our mother's journey and her mother's story (our gaka or grandma). A story built on tremendous faith, hope and pride. One that continues to be the wind that uplifts us every time we encounter a challenging situation as adults, for overcoming challenges would not be possible if our mother had not struggled and forged a path of infinite opportunities for us to attain. Reading our mother's story was an eye-opener.

We knew so little about her growing up. Yes, she talked about going to school barefooted and walking for miles and miles to get to her boarding school. But we did not realize that our grandma used to hoist our mother's suitcase on her head – nor did we know that our grandma read through our mother's eyes. As children, we take so much for granted and we just assume our mum got where she got by a blink of an eye. This clearly shows our grandma was our mother's first teacher. Though not all of us had a chance to meet our grandma – she is with us.

As Sein shares, "I never had the chance to meet my grandmother; however, I feel her spirit through my veins. I have been to her graveside many times. I have a reminder that I must continue to work hard and that I must teach my future children to dream big, and never stop challenging themselves. My mother's story brought moments of joy as I remembered the many nights I saw her typing away on her computer or the numerous goodbyes as she embarked on a conference in another country or the many nights she would come to my room to share her travel stories; the people she had met or the many challenging situations she had encountered at her place of work or even making sense of what it means to live in another country."

As for Nairesiae, she had many interesting things to say about her grandma:

"I remember Gaka as a warm woman, very caring and she made each of us feel special. I still cannot figure out how she did this because she had many grandchildren. Yet, every time we visited her, she had a special something for us. Also, I remember her as a woman who was always busy – just like our mother. She was always cooking some-thing in a big pot and I always looked forward to tasting her food, which tasted very different from the foods in the city. I guess that was because it was organic and it was cooked over a three-stone fire. I thought it was magical. Our grandparents' compound was special, there was a feeling of happiness – lots of laughter, playing under the stars and warming ourselves by the fire in the compound that my grandpa had prepared so that he could tell us stories. I cannot wait to take my daughters to visit their great-grandparents' homestead.

"As for my mother, reading her memoir, I have gotten to know her better. I got to understand what life in the village meant for a little girl. Her memoir gave me an opportunity to see her adventurous, mischievous side. This is because I thought of her as a busy mum, always wearing high heels, running around and seeing her daughter and her personality blossom. I see aspects of the mischievous, adventurous, fearless spirit that my mother has. This has made us aware of the connectedness of similarities of our lives whether growing up in the village in Kenya or in a city like Toronto."

Koyiet remembers his grandma very vividly:

"Gaka used to make me laugh. She had a special name for me – she called me Kajet. No one else ever called me that. Also, come to think of it, she was a healer. I remember one time she came to visit us in Nairobi and I was very sick with chicken pox. All that I remember was Gaka covering me with leaves and making me drink some bitter stuff, and then every morning she would hold a blanket over me and a steaming pot of herbs she had prepared. I would sweat – and sweat – after which she would instruct that I should be without clothes, and within two to three days, I was healed.

"I wish we knew what herbs she was using. The other thing I remember about Gaka was her generosity, and though she had so little, she always had something to give each one of us. It could have been a fruit or money; she was a loving grandma who truly cared for her grandchildren. She was very comforting to be around. Reading this book took me back to those moments and I realized what a great woman Gaka was.

"As for Mum, reading this book has shown me what it means for one to make a sacrifice for a better future. It never made sense to me; you left us early to go back to school. You were always reading books, doing homework from the time I can remember. I know Dad would also talk to us about your education, and many times he would say, 'Your mum needs to have an education, she has to have tools to hold the family together if I am not around.'

"Dad's words did not make sense to me – until now – after reading this book. You went to school because you had a dream; you went back to school because you were Gaka's eyes; you did not spend time away because you wanted to provide a better life for us; your sacrifice has brought discipline, structure, organization and independence into my life. In a way you do remind me of Gaka because you have a big heart; no matter what we do to you, no matter how much we have upset you, you are always there for us."

Our mother's story has given us moments of deep reflection, as we thought of the hardships of growing up in the village in Embu, but then, from the memoir, our mother appears to be a very happy child, playing, dreaming, imagining and even saying she wanted to be a professor. What? From the village, she wanted to be a professor – without even knowing what a professor did or looked like, or even her reflection of going to a boarding school that had little to nothing, yet it provided our mother the meditative spirit she displays when she lights her candles, burns her incense and sits in silence for hours – habits developed from long sessions of prayers in a Catholic boarding school.

Would we endure that as children? We are not sure. However, we believe we would. Our mother has a free spirit; that is not obvious to many, but it is there. We know it and when she lets her hair down, she is truly fun to be around. We have seen that happiness of being an African, carefree child untainted by the "modern" technology of cell phones, internet and television sitcoms. As an African woman, living so far from where she grew up, and teaching in one of the top universities in Canada as a full professor, this story brought immense pride to us because it was not just another story of "coming to the Americas," rather "coming from Africa." It was refreshing, heartfelt and one that has inspired us to one day write a story "from our mother's back" in dedication to her.

We love you, Mum.

Moody, Aziz, Sein, Nairesiae and Koyiet

ACKNOWLEDGEMENTS

There are so many people I would like to say asante sana for who I am or what I am, but first, I want to give thanks to my Creator, Mwene Nyaga, for the many blessings. To my university (University of Toronto), thank you for the space to express my intellectual curiosity. To my Canadian family (David and Inez, Grace and Basil, Yvette and Errol, Yama and Houston, Claude and Michelle, Tony and Rose, Vera and Thomas, Evelyn and Joseph). To my colleagues, thank you.

My family immediate and extended: What can I say? Each one of you means lots and lots to me. I truly love each one of you in very special ways. Although I might not show it or I have never said it out loud to you, I truly do. My brothers, sisters, nieces, nephews, my cousins, my grandnieces and grandnephews; I hold you dearly in my heart. You have showered me with so much love, material gifts, laughter and warmth. You have always been there for me. I come from a large family and I am worried that I might forget some names, however, I will try: Maina, you died too soon before I got to know you, but you left us with your wife and children. Brother Francis, although you are no longer with us, I still remember when you bought your first radio and we would all gather around it to listen to the voice from the tiny little box. Your family has been a blessing to us. Siporata, thank you – for carrying the suitcases for my brothers; and Anisia for your willingness to assist all those who require help and your beautiful voice. Sofia, still keeping strong, thank you. Mary Ndwiga, you taught me how to hold a fork and knife and how to be a good host, asante sana; thank you for sharing your family with us, and in particular Baba Robert, your husband provided extra tutoring so that we could pass national exams. Wanyiri, I still remember you before you got married, wearing a beautiful short dress with high heels – thank you for making me a flower girl; Kiringa: I still remember, you got married on a Wednesday and you had lots of rice and chapatti – thank you; Monika: thank you for being yourself. Brother Anthony, you were special and you will always remain special in my life; thank you for Mary Njagi, and your beautiful children. Brother Henry, thank you for all the information you shared with me as I wrote my memoir, you are our family historian and keeper of knowledge, although you are no longer with us, I will always treasure your words of wisdom. Emily, thank you for keeping everything intact, when Henry was away. Brother Njuki and your wife Njoki, thank you for being yourself and for sharing. Sister Mbere, thank you for holding my hand as we crossed the Ena River to go to school. Brother Mugeni, the family intellectual, and your wife Maggi, another intellectual, thank you for being who both are. Mugeni – don't forget you still owe me a pair of shoes – and Anisia for your beautiful voice.

Brother Njeru and your wife Edith, thank you. Njeru, my baby brother, thank you for making me laugh when the going is tough.

To my children, Koyiet, Nairesiae, Sein, Aziz and Moody, you are the ones who make me wake up every morning. If you did not know, I always think of you and thank God for you. Koyiet, you're the family warrior. Never forget that. Nairesiae, the organizer, cherish your gift and use it to your advantage. Sein, the family lawyer, we cherish your counsel. Aziz, your wisdom is beyond your years. Moody, you are our baby and have a special spot in our hearts. And to my Nanas, Jeavohn, Mikal, Sharissa, Shanice, Taiyana, Kaden, Emilia and Malaika, you are very special to me; you make my world rock.

And of course, to the love of my life, Amadou, I have no words to describe what you have done for me. Your family became my family. You have given me so much support to shine, that I could not have asked my Creator to give me a better husband and soulmate.

To my publisher Noelle, thank you for taking me through to the finishing line. Your counsel and wisdom has made my book the memoir I always wanted to write.

Njoki Nathani Wane, Ph.D., a professor at the University of Toronto, was the Special Advisor on the Status of Women at University of Toronto. Currently, she is the Chair of the Department of Social Justice Education at the Ontario Institute for Studies in Education (OISE), University of Toronto. She was born in Kenya.

Dr. Wane received her education both in Kenya and in North America. From 2009 to 2012, she was the Director of the Office of Teachers Support at OISE (OTSO). OTSO's central focus was to provide ongoing faculty development to the Ontario Institute for Studies in Education, University of Toronto's faculty and aspiring university graduate students. With a central focus on teaching, OTSO provided workshops, consultations and other professional development opportunities to the OISE community. In 2009, she was one of the TVO Ontario Nominees for Best Lecturer and in 2008, she received the Harry Jerome Professional Excellence Award. In 2007, she won the African Women Achievement Award. In 2016, she won the President's Teaching Award.

For the last twenty years, she has been researching, writing and teaching in the areas of Black feminisms in Canada and Africa and African Indigenous knowledge, as well as African women and spirituality.